D0436420

LET THEM SEE YOU

RRALS DOES NOT MEAN THA

RIMINATORY HIRING. IT'S M

F RELIANCE ON REFERRALS.

NIES' FINANCIAL PERFORMA

ED **THE GUIDE FOR** CAREER F

F WE'RE **LEVERAGING YOUR**

ET **DIVERSITY AT WORK**. WE

W. WE'VE GOT TO CONVINCE

PANIES THAT THEY NEED TO

IER THAN EXPECTING A QUA

AT TO THE TOP OF A CROWDE

W THEM THAT WE ARE HERE.

ELOPERS. WE'RE CFOS. IF WE

CAN—WE HAVE THE OPPORTU

ORCE FOR THE BETTER. IT'S

COMPANY IS ENGAGING IN
LY AN UNINTENDED CONSEQ
CAN **PORTER BRASWELL** IM
E **WITH RYAN GALLOWAY** IT
SPECTS OF PEOPLE OF COLO
INESSES AND OURSELVES, W
GOT TO CHANGE HOW BUSIN
E DECISION-MAKERS AT OUR
TIVELY SEARCH FOR DIVERSE
ED PERSON OF COLOR TO M
PPLICANT POOL. WE'VE GOT
'RE MARKETERS. WE'RE SOF
N WORK TOGETHER—AND I
Y TO CHANGE THE FACE OF
E TO

LET THEM SEE YOU.

LORENA JONES BOOKS
California | New York

CONTENTS

A Time to Lead

PROLOGUE

I'm Porter Braswell, the CEO and cofounder of a company called Jopwell, a technology platform that helps Black, Latinx, and Native American students and professionals unlock opportunities for career advancement. Under my leadership, Jopwell has formed partnerships with more than one hundred of America's leading companies and has facilitated tens of thousands of connections between the Jopwell community members and our clients. To date, we've raised more than $11.5 million from the likes of Magic Johnson, Andreessen Horowitz, Y Combinator, Kapor Capital, Cue Ball, and others.

Since we founded Jopwell in 2015, the company has been recognized by *Entrepreneur* magazine (100 Most Brilliant Ideas), *Fast Company* (World's Most Innovative Companies), and *Business Insider* (One of the Hottest New York City Companies to Watch). Over the years, I've received professional awards and recognition that include being named to LinkedIn's Next Wave: Top Professionals 35 and Under, *Inc.* magazine's 30 Under 30, *Fast Company*'s 100 Most Creative People In Business, Crain's 40 Under 40, *Vanity Fair*'s Future Innovators Index, and *Adweek*'s Young Influencers (the publication's annual list of the most innovative minds under age 40).

Before Jopwell, I worked at Goldman Sachs, buying and selling currencies. Before Goldman Sachs, I attended Yale University, where I was a member of the men's varsity basketball team. Working at Goldman Sachs was everything my family had envisioned for me. My father, born in the Bronx with very few resources, became general counsel for a publicly traded utility company and, eventually, a New Jersey state judge. My mother, raised in the suburbs of New York in Westchester County, was an elementary school teacher in the inner city of East Orange, New Jersey. My parents worked so hard to give me access to a great education, and working in the financial industry was their dream for me. But it wasn't my dream. Grateful as I was to them, I wanted more.

In spite of my education, there are many factors that should have led to the failure of Jopwell by now:

1. I'm a Black male, which means I belong to a group that gets less than 1% of venture captial money despite African-Americans making up 11% of the U.S. population. Additionally, all-Black founding teams raise almost half as much money compared to all-white founding teams.
2. I'm nontechnical, and so is my cofounder, Ryan. Tech companies that don't have a technical founder are almost always destined for failure.
3. I had never started a business before.
4. I was only twenty-seven when we launched Jopwell.
5. I quit an incredibly desirable job, and so did my partner; giving up and going back to finance would have been much easier.

I've written this book because I want to significantly expand the conversation about diversity in the workplace. I believe in the power of technology to change this issue, though I know that there are no easy answers. We've all seen headlines like these:

> *Forbes*: "Apple CEO Tim Cook Is 'Not Satisfied' with Employee Diversity"
>
> *The Guardian*: "Why Are 'Innovative' Tech Companies Still Struggling with Diversity?"
>
> *TechCrunch*: "It's True, Black Female Founders Receive Basically Zero Venture Capital"

I know that many companies are hungry to hire diverse candidates and that the lack of diversity is a problem they care about and feel responsible for changing. Diversity is also good for business. But our national conversation about this subject is stuck in a rut.

To start to change that, I'm going to share the success stories of others as well as my own. This book will bring you face to face with real-world strategies for overcoming common obstacles for people of color, and it will also teach you the lessons that I've learned from some of my influential mentors, including people such as Magic Johnson (NBA legend and NBA Hall of Fame inductee) and Mitch and Freada Kapor (VC investors and activists in the field of organizational culture and diversity).

When we first started Jopwell, we intentionally decided not to refer to our community as "diverse." We felt this diluted our mission and, instead, we decided to refer to our community as "Black, Latinx, and Native American." Even with this specification, we understood that racial and cultural identity is complicated, varied, and personal. We use the word "Black" to capture the many and very different cultures that fit underneath the umbrella term. In the same vein, we use the term "Latinx" so we can be as inclusive as possible to all identities in that spectrum. We believe that in America, being

Black creates shared experiences for all those who identify as such. At the start of 2017, we changed from using "Latino" to Latinx as we wanted to be gender neutral and more progressive in the way we discussed our population.

Throughout the book, I've used the term "people of color," or POC, because, in corporate America, the most underrepresented groups are POC. While POC is an umbrella term that doesn't allow us to discuss the nuances of each unique culture, it does allow for a dialogue detailing practical advice that minorities can implement and leverage in the workplace to realize their potential. As a Black American male, I, too, would rather not be categorized under such large umbrella terms, but for the purpose of this book and in order to provide the most practical advice to the largest audience that historically hasn't been "seen" in the workplace, I use the term POC.

The practical advice presented throughout this book is meant to help you overcome challenges and obstacles that arise while working with naive and sheltered colleagues—not racist colleagues. Racism still exists—in all locations. If you don't believe me, read my LinkedIn post on what happened to me on my subway ride home in New York City (linkedin.com/pulse/things-still-happen-porter-braswell).

It's important to call this out now because, again, as a Black man, I have experienced racism and also dealt with ill-informed and yet not intentionally malicious colleagues. It's important to know the difference. You have to find a way to thrive in environments where your peers just don't seem to get it. It will make you a stronger person, a better leader, and a more effective mentor. In environments where you are dealing with racism, you have to speak up and speak out against it. The challenge is being able to identify what's ignorance and what's racism, which I trust you'll be able to do as I have and still do. The advice in the book will also assist in that process.

We're each born with an internal compass that directs us to what we're meant to do. We all want a purpose. Some people recognize that purpose as a calling, a deep sense of responsibility, or an unsettling feeling that makes them scared they're not living up to their potential. Whatever you name it, that *thing* is something we all have and feel. When we are able to follow that compass, movements are created, businesses are built and reengineered, corporate ladders are climbed, and leaders emerge.

INTRODUCTION

Like many women of color who choose to wear their hair naturally, Chelsea Johnson often encounters uninvited criticism from her colleagues and peers about her hair. They've called it "wild," "unprofessional," "masculine," and even just "ugly." In response, she's done what many professionals of color often do when faced with insensitivity in the workplace: she has taken a breath and done her best to educate her coworkers.

Chelsea's hardly alone. POC in the workforce are reminded daily that we're different from most of our coworkers. The vast majority of those reminders are unintentional, and the speakers rarely intend to be insensitive. Often they're cloaked in positivity. I'd need a few dozen hands to count the number of times I've been told how "articulate" and "well-spoken" I am. But even though the speaker thought they were paying me a compliment, I felt as if they'd assumed I *wouldn't* be articulate, which is alarming.

Every time it happened, it chipped a little piece of me away. It made me a little less engaged at work. It made me a little less likely to go above and beyond. And it kept me from referring diverse professionals from my network to positions at my company. Instead of bringing in more people from my community, I felt as if I was doing my friends and relatives a favor by keeping them out.

From my conversations with Chelsea and countless other professionals of color, I know my experience is not unique. But the vast majority of the companies we work for and the colleagues with whom we work aren't deliberately trying to make us feel like outsiders. After all, companies around the United States spend billions of dollars every year on diversity hiring initiatives. But these programs are rarely effective, leaving people like Chelsea and me—and quite possibly you, too—with workplaces in which we're a very underrepresented minority.

And it's not just POC who suffer when diversity programs fail. Companies suffer as well. Their reputations as employers can be tarnished, they can make costly messaging mistakes when trying to reach our communities, and, perhaps most important, they underperform financially.

That's why I cofounded Jopwell, and it's why I wrote this book. It's about fixing what's fundamentally wrong with how we think about diversity recruitment—and how we, professionals of color, can do that together. In fact, we're the only ones who can do it at all.

But this book isn't just for POC. It isn't directed at recruiters, heads of human resources, and chief diversity officers. It's actually intended for every professional who's passionate about building a more inclusive, representational workforce and reaping the financial and performance rewards that come with it.

But before we go any further, let's be clear about what diversity means to us.

Many of the diversity challenges that companies face stem from the fact that they can't articulate what "diversity" is. Some focus on ethnicity only. Others incorporate gender, sexual orientation, socioeconomic background, and education level. Often the definition widens to the point that it comes to include anyone who isn't a straight white man. This lack of focus ultimately prevents organizations from crafting smart, actionable plans to attack the problem at hand.

After countless conversations, the best definition I've found for what companies are looking for is diversity of experience. The person who's being described as "diverse" has experienced the world differently from the majority of the workforce. For example, because I'm a Black man in the United States, my experiences differ from those of my white colleagues, even if we grew up in the same town, have the same sexual orientation, went to the same college, and have the same job.

When we founded Jopwell, we used ethnicity to define diversity. We knew it wasn't perfect, but we had two pretty good reasons for choosing this rationale.

The first reason is simple: POC are the most traditionally underrepresented groups in the American workforce. From Jim Crow to the current president's repeated vilification of Hispanic immigrants, we've been up against powerful opponents to claim our place in the American workforce. We're still fighting, but today our primary opponent is the corporate world's unwillingness to see us and seek us out. Despite seismic changes in demographics, increasing post-secondary educational attainment, and the billions of dollars that companies sink into recruiting diverse professionals each year, we're still struggling to find our place in offices around the country.

Consider this: POC make up 30% of the total workforce, but we're far less likely to hold the kinds of jobs that the Bureau of Labor statistics calls "professional"—management, technology, and knowledge-based jobs, like accounting and human resources. We account for only 18% of those jobs, far fewer than whites and Asians. Another sobering statistic? Just 20% of Hispanics and 30% of Blacks at work today hold "professional" jobs, compared to 40% of whites and 50% of Asians.[1]

The second reason is that narrowing Jopwell's definition of diversity allows the company to focus on a specific set of professionals and put all our resources and expertise into elevating their profiles and helping them get the attention they deserve. It doesn't mean Jopwell has actively excluded other ethnicities or isn't sensitive to the struggles of other diverse communities. But there are other organizations out there who can have—and are having—a bigger impact for these communities than Jopwell ever could.

Defining diversity is just the first step in addressing what ails countless companies around the country. To build a truly diverse workforce, companies have to stop relying on referrals and seek help from the communities they're trying to reach.

I've talked to hundreds of recruiters and chief diversity officers over the past few years, and almost all of them have told me that they don't get enough applicants from diverse backgrounds.

Yet, almost a quarter of all bachelor's degrees are granted to POC every year.[2] Nearly 20% of all bachelor's degrees in STEM fields were earned by Black and Hispanic students in 2012 alone.[3] Shouldn't this mean that at least 20% of the applicant pipeline for almost any entry-level gig in the tech field consist of POC? And if the top of the recruiting funnel is diverse, shouldn't the bottom be diverse as well?

The answer, of course, is yes. But the real problem is that these companies are looking in the wrong place—if they're looking at all.

You see, it's the word "applicants" that causes many companies to stumble. Many of the major job boards allow job seekers to apply to jobs en masse with just a few clicks. By allowing an uncurated and unlimited number of people to apply to positions for which they're unqualified, they've effectively turned recruiters' talent pools into a spam folder. That's why, in a 2017 study, 80% of employers reported that their biggest barrier to identifying qualified talent was "too many unqualified, junk résumés from job boards."[4]

Understandably, recruiters then often turn to another source of talent: referrals from current employees. Recent research has revealed that referrals make up just 7% of employers' applicant pools but account for 40% of total hires. And nearly nine out of ten recruiters say they believe referrals are the best source for a quality candidate.[5] And therein lies the problem.

Yes, referrals are a great source of talent. But they're also a great source of sameness. Think about it: whom do we refer? Our friends, our family members, and members of our communities. These people are overwhelmingly likely to share our ethnic, socioeconomic, and even geographic backgrounds.

Let's start from the moment a company is founded. A 2015 study by VC research firm CBInsights found that 87% of startup founders were white.[6] And I know from personal experience that when you are founding a company, your earliest employees have to be trusted partners who share your vision and values. So you turn to the people you trust—friends, family, former colleagues—for referrals. If you and your cofounders are white, then your early employees are likely to be white as well. In fact, 40% of white Americans and 25% of non-white Americans have no friends outside their own race.[7] So, as your business grows over time, the likelihood of your employees referring POC becomes vanishingly small.

A friend of mine—we'll call him Sam—has spent almost his entire career with a Manhattan-based engineering and urban planning consultancy. Most of the engineers who were initially hired were Pakistani. Many of the planners were Black or Asian. Because the company was small and specialized, they relied heavily on referrals to grow. As the company grew, something fascinating happened: it became extraordinarily diverse and stayed that way. Today, the company that began with a small office in Chelsea has hundreds of employees who have roots in more than twenty countries. It's a case study in the performance benefits that come from having a diverse workforce. Much of what makes diversity so effective in the business world is the range of experiences and perspectives that people from different backgrounds contribute. It's why companies with highly diverse workforces are 35% more likely to financially outperform their less diverse competitors.[8]

Late in 2016, Snap Inc., the company behind the popular Snapchat app, filed the paperwork for its highly anticipated IPO. In it, they included a note about diversity. The note got a lot of things right, but it also defended the company's decision not to follow its Silicon Valley counterparts in releasing a diversity report. "That's because we believe diversity is about more than numbers," the note read. And they're right. Diversity is about more than numbers.[9]

But numbers help.

In Snap's case, those numbers could have prevented a public relations disaster. If their leadership team had been composed at least partially of POC, it's highly unlikely that they would've released a filter that claimed to honor reggae legend Bob Marley by letting users see themselves with dreadlocks, a brightly colored rasta cap—and Black skin.[10]

Almost immediately, Twitter users began criticizing Snap for enabling what is essentially digital blackface. Shortly thereafter, the company released a statement, saying: "Millions of Snapchatters have enjoyed Bob Marley's music, and we respect his life and achievements," and that the filter gave "people a new way to share their appreciation for Bob Marley and his music."

Another PR disaster occurred just a few months later, when Pepsi debuted its now-infamous "Live for Now Moments" commercial, featuring reality star Kendall Jenner. In it, Jenner sees a protest passing by while she models for a photo shoot. She's so moved by this protest that she removes her wig, joins in, and eventually defuses tension by handing a police officer a Pepsi.

Almost instantly, Twitter exploded with accusations that the commercial was attempting to co-opt and trivialize the Black Lives Matter movement. Less than twenty-four hours later, Pepsi pulled the ad and issued an apology, stating: "Pepsi was trying to project a global message of unity, peace and understanding. Clearly, we missed the mark and apologize."[11]

The list of products and ad campaigns that have failed due to cultural insensitivity and corporate tone deafness could fill an entire book. My point is not that companies often fail when trying to reach and engage diverse communities. My point is that these companies fail to reach us for the same reason they fail to find us during the hiring process: they're trying to do it themselves without input from the people they want to attract.

Did the Snap team intentionally set out to create a blackface filter? Of course not. Nor did Pepsi knowingly trivialize Black Lives Matter. I'm confident that both companies genuinely had no idea that these efforts would be offensive, likely because there weren't enough—or possibly any—POC sitting at the table when the content was conceived or approved.

It's a safe bet that Snap is keenly aware of their diversity issue. They employ an inclusion and diversity recruitment manager, and a chief diversity officer is probably soon to join. These are certainly steps in the right direction. But if the rest of Snap's technology peers are any example, these steps are just the first in a long and difficult journey.

Relying on referrals does not mean that a company is engaging in discriminatory hiring. It's merely an unintended consequence of reliance on referrals. But it can have a seismic impact on companies' financial performance down the line, and it dramatically limits the career prospects of POC.

If we're going to help businesses and ourselves, we've got to disrupt this process. We've got to change how businesses grow. We've got to convince the decision-makers at our companies that they need to actively search for diverse talent, rather than expecting qualified POC to magically float to the top of a crowded applicant pool.

We have to show them that we are here. We're marketers. We're software developers. We're CFOs. If we can work together—and I believe we can—we have the opportunity to change the face of the American workforce for the better.

It's time to let them see you.

THE MOVEMENT

1

THE BUSINESS CASE FOR DIVERSITY

The Data and History behind a More Diverse Workforce

When Candice Morgan joined Pinterest, one of the fastest-growing Silicon Valley–based companies, as its first head of inclusion and diversity, she knew that the young company had a workforce makeup similar to many of its peers. The company was 49% white and 43% Asian. Hispanic or Latinx employees were just 2% of the staff, and only 1% were Black. At the leadership level, Hispanic, Latinx, Black, and Native American professionals were absent entirely.[12]

Candice, who had come from a decade-long tenure at nonprofit Catalyst, clearly had a steep hill to climb. But she also had something that many change makers can only dream of: allies at the founder level.

Pinterest's founders, Evan Sharp and Ben Silbermann, have been among Silicon Valley's most vocal advocates of diversity since 2015. The company has been at the forefront of the movement to share diversity data and publicly address plans to tackle their hiring woes.

And with Candice joining in January of 2016, they doubled down on their efforts to right the ship.

They started by setting hiring goals and publicizing them. At the end of the year, they were candid about their performance against those goals. In the course of a year, they more than doubled the number of employees from underrepresented minorities and increased the number of engineers from those minority communities to 9% of the overall engineering staff, a dramatic increase from a dismal starting point of just 1%. Likewise, the percentage of new hires who were new engineering graduates went from 2% to 9%, and nearly 20% of all engineering interns were from underrepresented groups. And in nonengineering roles, the percentage of underrepresented minorities hired grew to 12% from 7% the previous year.[13]

These gains are great, and they're a clear sign that Candice and the team at Pinterest are doing something right. But from a business standpoint, is all of this investment of time and resources really worth it? When a company is performing as well as Pinterest is, is it really wise to pump dollars into recruiting people from diverse backgrounds?

Yes, it is. You see, building a diverse workforce is an investment that delivers tangible benefits. But many companies are still failing to grasp this.

Miscommunications and Misconceptions: How We Got Here

Skepticism about the validity of diversity hiring programs is nothing new. It has existed for as long as the programs themselves (and they have been around longer than you may realize). Still, today, there are murmurings in the halls of some of the most progressive companies that the time and resources dedicated to diversity hiring initiatives are wasted.

"It's a feel-good thing," some say.

"We just had a Black president for eight years," say others. "Isn't that a clear sign that diversity isn't a problem anymore?"

I've heard more permutations of these statements than I can recall, but the one I've heard most often is, "Shouldn't we just focus on hiring the best person for the job? Who cares what ethnicity they are?"

Many—including some of today's smartest and most progressive business leaders—still cling to these assumptions because of *messaging.*

To understand how messaging plays the lead role in the entrenched misunderstanding of American diversity initiatives, we've got to go back to the start of those initiatives. For our purposes, that's the year 1921.

FORD, FDR, AND THE ORIGINS OF DIVERSITY INITIATIVES IN THE UNITED STATES

In the years immediately following World War I, the automotive market boomed in the United States. To meet the growing demand for new cars, in 1917, the Ford Motor Company began construction on a massive new factory in Dearborn, Michigan. But the economy soon slowed, and by 1921, Ford was faced with the prospect of sizable layoffs at its new facility.

After hearing the news, leaders of the Black community approached Henry Ford, the company's founder, and asked him to not dismiss a disproportionate number of Black workers. After all, Ford employed thousands of skilled Black workers, and a massive layoff would be a disaster for Detroit's Black community. Ford agreed and did as they asked. And then he did something unprecedented.

Following the layoffs, Ford created a policy stating that the percentage of Black workers in the company's workforce should directly correspond to the percentage of Black people within Detroit's population. The policy also stated that Blacks should be represented in

TRUST BUT VERIFY

Ford's policy of hiring Black professionals to oversee and enforce inclusive hiring practices showed amazing foresight. Not only was management more capable of finding and attracting workers of color, but they were also inherently more invested in the success of the program than in the success of their individual colleagues. A policy without enforcement infrastructure is destined for failure.

all departments of the company, and Ford appointed Black officials within the company's personnel department specifically tasked with hiring Black people and ensuring that discriminatory hiring practices didn't occur.[14]

I cannot overstate how revolutionary this step was. In a time when discrimination was the norm and segregation was the law, Ford made diversity hiring both mandatory and enforceable. This program was also likely the inspiration for the first national diversity hiring program—which, sadly, would not be established for twelve more years.

By 1933, the Great Depression had taken a powerful toll on the American workforce. The unemployment rate for that year, a staggering 25%, remains the highest rate registered in American history. With thirteen million people out of work, times were dire for people from all walks of life. POC, however, were hit especially hard. Discrimination was the norm in almost every industry, and when jobs were available, POC were the last to be considered—if they were considered at all. In fact, the 1930 census showed that, in some regions of the United States, the unemployment rate was 80% higher for African-Americans than it was for whites.[15]

The New Deal, President Franklin D. Roosevelt's response to the nation's economic crisis, was revolutionary. The programs it created gave millions of Americans jobs and opportunities to learn valuable skills. But just as revolutionary was an order issued by Harold Ickes. As the secretary of the interior, Ickes was in charge of implementing much of the New Deal and served as the head of its major relief program, the Works Progress Administration (WPA). Ickes's order, issued in 1933, created what was essentially the first program that enforced diversity in hiring.[16]

The order itself simply prohibited discrimination in hiring for WPA projects. That may seem like small potatoes today, but at the time, it was unprecedented. And the very next year, two of Ickes's aides, Robert Weaver and Clark Foreman, took another significant step forward by creating what would become the forerunner of affirmative action. Contractors in cities with an "appreciable" population of African-Americans were required to hire a fixed percentage of skilled Black workers. That percentage was one-half of the number of skilled Black workers in the overall labor force. In Atlanta, for example, skilled Black workers made up around 24% of the total labor force, so WPA contractors would have to prove that 12% of their total payrolls consisted of Black workers.[17]

The WPA's quota system was the first of its kind, and it was a major step forward for diversity hiring in the United States. Unfortunately—and predictably—once put into practice it wasn't terribly successful. The quota system was nearly impossible to enforce, and many contractors either ignored the policy altogether or circumvented it by hiring the requisite number of Black workers, only to fire them once federal funding was received. Ickes and his colleagues also failed to craft messaging that conveyed *why* the policy existed and how a more diverse workforce would benefit the contractors themselves. Even if they had, however, it would likely have done little good. It was an idea whose time had come, but the majority of Americans just weren't ready for it.

THE IMPACT OF WORLD WAR II ON DIVERSITY

Americans still weren't ready in 1941. The Second World War raged around the globe, and while the United States had not yet formally entered the war, many government officials, including President Roosevelt, believed it was only a matter of time before the country would be forced to fight. His administration had spent the preceding year preparing for war by doubling the size of the U.S. Navy and urging Congress to approve the country's first peacetime military draft.

Discrimination and segregation were the norm in almost every industry, and the defense industry, busy with preparations for war and hiring on an unprecedented scale, was no exception. For white Americans, the defense industry's boom provided a welcome change from the dire conditions of the Great Depression. For POC, however, the doors of the defense industry remained closed. Even those people with highly desirable skills faced discrimination.

Meanwhile, the federal government was issuing calls for all Americans to "defend democracy" and resist the racism of Nazi ideology calls. For POC, these calls rang especially hollow due to the entrenched racism they faced at work and in their communities. For civil rights leaders A. J. Muste, A. Philip Randolph, and Bayard Rustin, this growing resentment, combined with the defense industry's continued segregation—despite its urgent need for skilled workers—was a powerful lever for change.

Together, Muste, Randolph, and Rustin proposed a massive march on Washington. Faced with the possibility of 50,000 demonstrators coming together in the nation's capital, President Roosevelt quickly caved in to the pressure. In June of 1941, just six months before the attack on Pearl Harbor that would finally bring the United States into

BE THE CHANGE

Today, Ford, FDR, Truman, and Ickes get most of the credit for creating the revolutionary policies of the forties. But none of them would have happened if POC hadn't taken the initiative and made their voices heard. Don't wait for leadership to make a change just because it's the right thing to do. Take charge and be the change you want to see in your organization.

the war, he issued Executive Order 8802, which prohibited discriminatory hiring practices in the defense industry. It read, in part:

> *Whereas it is the policy of the United States to encourage full participation in the national defense program by all citizens of the United States, regardless of race, creed, color, or national origin, in the firm belief that the democratic way of life within the Nation can be defended successfully only with the help and support of all groups within its borders.*[18]

The impact that Randolph and his fellow civil rights leaders had on this decision can't be overstated. But President Roosevelt was an extremely progressive politician for the time and generally enjoyed positive relations with civil rights leaders. I strongly suspect he was aware that, if the United States was to be its most effective in the war that was sure to come, the defense industry would need to engage the skills, talents, and perspectives of Americans of every race and ethnic background.

And—let's be honest—Randolph probably knew a policy change wasn't going to happen organically. Regardless of his motivations, the order was the first action taken by the U.S. government to ban employment discrimination in any industry, and it's where the history of diversity programs in the United States begins. It was also, as you might imagine, not well received by everyone. Remember, this was an America where institutionalized racism was visible in nearly every aspect of daily life—and a few of its citizens could even remember being enslaved. But faced with the looming need to wage war on a global scale, the country couldn't afford for its defense industry to remain exclusively white.

The war itself, coming just six months after the order was issued, brought together people from diverse backgrounds on an unprecedented scale. However, the armed forces remained segregated throughout the war itself, with Black soldiers typically serving in support roles, like cooking, cleaning, and vehicle maintenance, due to the prevailing view that they would be inferior to white soldiers in combat. But as the war progressed, personnel shortages forced military leaders to deploy all-Black units in combat. Those leaders soon found that, contrary to their preexisting biases, all-Black units performed just as well as—and, in some cases, better than—their exclusively white counterparts.

The exceptional performance of units like the Tuskegee Airmen of the 332nd Fighter Group, the 477th Bombardment Group, and the Black Panthers of the 761st Tank Battalion, for example, forced military leaders and the public alike to confront their biases and misguided beliefs about the capabilities of Black soldiers. But for the rank-and-file soldiers themselves, simply serving alongside Black soldiers was often enough to fight misconceptions about race.

In fact, a 1945 survey of white soldiers and officers commissioned by the President's Committee on Equality of Treatment and Opportunity in the Armed Services found that 64% had initially disliked being assigned to a company with both white and Black platoons. But when asked if their views about Black soldiers had improved during the course of the war, 77% said they had.[19]

The policy shift also afforded military and government leaders an opportunity to realize something that some business leaders still can't wrap their heads around: diverse teams really do perform better.

That's why, in 1948, yet another executive order desegregated the armed forces altogether. Executive Order 9981, this time issued by President Truman, proclaimed:

> *"It is hereby declared to be the policy of the President that there shall be equality of treatment and opportunity for all persons in the armed services without regard to race, color, religion or national origin. This policy shall be put into effect as rapidly as possible, having due regard to the time required to effectuate any necessary changes without impairing efficiency or morale."*[20]

Again, the order did not go over well with all parties, and it took years for the military to truly integrate servicemen and -women of all ethnic backgrounds. But these two executive actions were the key steps on the long road toward ending segregation and discrimination in the United States—and they came about as a result of actions taken by POC and the realization that diversity has a measurable, positive impact on performance.

What we see here are the results of what may be the first real business case for diversity. Not only did the U.S. government and its military leaders find real and immediate value in promoting diversity, but they also took the risky and largely unpopular move of making diversity a practice. However, it would take nearly two decades and more government action for corporate America to begin catching up.

WHEN "DO THE RIGHT THING" IS THE WRONG MESSAGE

In an era when racism was the norm, the programs and policies put in place by Ford, FDR, and Ickes were truly revolutionary, but the messaging that accompanied them was woefully ineffective. Today, we can all agree that ending discrimination against POC was the right thing to do. In the early twentieth century, however, most Americans disagreed. These policies essentially said: "Do it because we say so." Unsurprisingly, many rejected this message, viewing it as the government's "telling them what to think."

A better choice would have been to explain to business owners and service people that diverse perspectives strengthen organizations rather than weaken them. A message focused on performance and effectiveness would have been more compelling than simply requiring them to do something they didn't believe in. When companies discuss diversity with the people in its organization, they need to make it about the business, not a moral obligation.

PROGRESS DURING THE CIVIL RIGHTS ERA

The next major landmark in diversity and inclusion was yet another executive order, this time issued by President John F. Kennedy on March 6, 1961. Executive Order 10925 required government contractors to "take affirmative action to ensure that applicants are employed and that employees are treated during employment without regard to their race, creed, color, or national origin."[21]

Like Roosevelt's order twenty years before, this was a small step focusing on employers doing work for or related to the U.S. government. Both orders may seem small in scope today, but they were both using government-related employers as a sort of test bed for broader acts. In the software industry, we call this "user testing." These orders are quite like the beta version of an app or software platform, an early version of a product introduced to a limited number of users to gauge reactions, find bugs, and evaluate viability before bringing a final product to market.

In the case of civil rights legislation, the final product would be released three years later. I'm speaking, of course, of the Civil Rights Act of 1964.[22] Like the World War II–era executive orders, the

1964 Act was a response to demonstrations by POC and their allies, particularly the Birmingham campaign undertaken by Martin Luther King Jr.'s Southern Christian Leadership Conference (SCLC).

In the early 1960s, Birmingham, Alabama, embodied America's racist history. Segregation of schools, public facilities like restaurants and hotels, and even buses was enforced, often through brutal means. But the SCLC's campaign of nonviolent protests in Birmingham and elsewhere brought discrimination and segregation into the national—and international—spotlight. With public opinion about America's institutional racism rapidly changing, both at home and abroad, President John F. Kennedy seized the moment.

From behind his desk in the Oval Office, Kennedy delivered a speech known as the Report to the American People on Civil Rights. The televised address, which lasted just over thirteen minutes, carefully laid out the moral and economic cases for civil rights and prepared the groundwork for the legislation to come. On June 19, eight days after the address, Kennedy sent his bill to Congress.[23] Six months later, he was assassinated in Dallas, Texas.

Kennedy's assassination could have dealt a crippling blow to the Civil Rights Act's success, but Lyndon Johnson, Kennedy's successor, took up the cause and shepherded the bill through Congress. On July 2, 1964, the bill was signed into law, and the landscape of the American workplace was changed forever.[24]

The act fundamentally changed the American workplace as it made racial discrimination, the norm in the United States since the country was founded, immediately and completely illegal. It outlawed racial discrimination in public places, like hotels, theaters, and restaurants, and it affected voting rights for POC and women's rights. But some of its most groundbreaking aspects were those in Title VII of the bill. That section made it illegal for employers with more than fifteen employees to discriminate based on race, color, religion, sex, or national origin. And it wasn't limited to hiring.

MAKE YOUR MESSAGE MATTER

It would've been easy for JFK's administration to buy up ad space in major newspapers and magazines and simply publicize his civil rights message in print. But by getting airtime on network TV that disrupted scheduled programming, Kennedy made it clear that his message was critically important. The medium also allowed him to convey his passion for the act in the most direct and engaging fashion. This is true for professionals at every level. When your message matters most, be selective about the forum you use to convey it. Make sure you choose a forum or a medium that guarantees attention and encourages engagement.

The section prohibited employers from engaging in discrimination during training, termination, promotion, compensation, and virtually every other facet of employment.[25]

Unsurprisingly, most companies were not equipped to deal with these changes. Their hiring practices and processes had to change quite literally overnight. While small companies could adapt relatively quickly, large companies could not. Recruiting and human resources professionals would have to be trained on those new standards, often more than once. Companies with locations in many states would have had an especially significant challenge rolling out changes to be compliant with Title VII, due in part to the number of people involved, but also to heavily entrenched racial biases in areas like the Deep South. In short, while the Civil Rights Act of 1964 was a watershed moment for POC in the United States, it was a logistical and human resources nightmare for large companies struggling to become compliant quickly.

DON'T GET DERAILED

After Kennedy's and Dr. Martin Luther King's deaths, the Civil Rights Act could've died on the vine. But Johnson took up the cause and was relentless in getting the act through Congress. Again, this conveyed the act's importance to other members of the government and to the American people. What could have been a major setback was overcome through hard work and perseverance. Major change is always met with resistance, but don't quit when the odds are stacked against you.

To get an idea of the scope of this challenge, imagine you're the CEO of a large national company with fifty thousand employees at thirty work sites across twenty-one states. Not only must you now ensure that every recruiter and hiring manager in your organization isn't engaging in discrimination—including asking potentially discriminatory questions during job interviews and the like—but you also must make sure your rank-and-file employees, many of whom may harbor racist beliefs, aren't acting or speaking in a way that could be deemed discriminatory during the regular working day. Suddenly, you're responsible for changing how thousands of people speak and behave for eight hours a day, five days a week. This is still a challenge for companies today, in fact. Recently, we read that more than a hundred Black employees of Tesla, Inc., had routinely faced racist behavior on the factory floor.[26]

In the sixties, business leaders weren't policing their employees' behavior just because it was now the law (and also, you know, just the right thing to do). In addition to bad press and negative impacts to public opinion, violating the Civil Rights Act could have measurable financial implications for a business's bottom line. During the sixties and seventies, many POC successfully sought redress for discrimination through use of the legal protections afforded to them under the act by filing discrimination lawsuits with the Equal Employment Opportunity Commission (EEOC). These lawsuits could result in costly fines or, more often, federally mandated diversity and inclusion trainings for management and staff.

To avoid these lawsuits, businesses had to become proactive about training their employees on diversity and inclusion. While the C-suite at some companies, such as IBM and Xerox, viewed diversity and inclusion as moral imperatives critical to ensuring a happy and productive workplace, most executives viewed them as a costly and unproductive nuisance. As a result, the time and resources dedicated to these training sessions were often minimal at best.

Some were as short as an hour, and many were one-time events, clearly designed to do nothing more than check off a box. Employees would be required to sign documents stating that they had attended the training as required and understood the costs and penalties associated with violating Title VII. After that, they were free to return to work—and they rarely left happy.

A 2008 article by Rohini Anand and Mary-Frances Winters in the *Academy of Management Learning & Education* perfectly sums up the common reactions to diversity and inclusion training:

> *Recipients of the early antidiscrimination training often left with a variety of emotions, few of them positive. Because the training focused primarily on treating historically underrepresented minorities and women fairly and equitably in White male-dominated environments and on avoidance of lawsuits, nonmembers of these groups resented their exclusion and felt that preferential treatment was being afforded to the targeted groups.*
>
> *Another reason that the training did not resonate well with the dominant group is that the content made little connection to*

> *how the recommended changes in behavior would improve business results. Although the late Kaleel Jamison, founder of the Kaleel Jamison Consulting Group, outlined the need to transform organizational culture, policies, practices and structures to create work environments that allow all employees to do their best work (Jamison, 1978), it would be a full decade before companies earnestly considered the role of inclusive organizational cultures as key drivers for the success of diversity efforts.*[27]

The Kaleel Jamison article referenced in the preceding extract, "Affirmative Action Program: Springboard for a Total Organizational Change Effort," ran in the popular organization development journal *OD Practitioner*.[28] Unfortunately, too few decision-makers took notice. As Anand and Winters noted, it took another decade for her ideas to start trickling into the mainstream.

FLIP THE SCRIPT

While the lawsuits that arose out of Title VII were necessary for holding companies accountable, they also instilled a palpable fear in business leaders, as monetary losses and public embarrassment were very real possibilities. Today, the message isn't about compliance; it's about creating more effective businesses by building more diverse teams. When you talk about diversity with the leaders of your organization, make that crystal clear. Today, the threat isn't just lawsuits—it's underperformance.

The Era of (In)Sensitivity Training

From the late seventies through the early eighties, diversity and inclusion programs pivoted away from enforcing compliance and toward enforcing assimilation. As more women and POC entered the professional workforce, companies created training programs designed to help these new entrants conform to their company's preexisting cultures and norms. In essence, they were "how to be more like us" programs. As we know today, this is exactly the opposite of how companies should approach diversity. It's also a terrific way to create an unproductive workplace and generate high levels of employee turnover.

Many organizations learned these lessons the hard way during the eighties—and, amazingly, some are still learning them. But in 1987, something happened that would fundamentally reshape the way businesses think about diversity and inclusion.

That something was a book called *Workforce 2000*.

Produced by the Hudson Institute, a nonprofit research organization, *Workforce 2000* showcased America's changing workforce in exhaustive detail. For business leaders, one of the key takeaways from the book was that, in the very near future, POC were going to be entering the workforce in higher numbers than ever before. Another discovery was that employers would have to actively hire POC to replace a majority white workforce that was aging and shrinking. The book also introduced the concept of "workforce diversity" as we know it today.

In response, businesses began changing diversity and inclusion trainings once again. This time, the training programs focused on sensitivity toward different cultures and customs. Unfortunately, the earliest of these programs explicitly told white men, who made up the majority within most organizations, that they had no valid issues worth discussing when it came to their experiences in the workplace. They were "the problem," and these programs were the solution.[29]

Undoubtedly, some of those men held racist attitudes and behaved insensitively at work. But these programs were often mandatory for all employees, and every white guy, no matter what his views were or what his behavior had been, received the same message. In their most extreme forms, the trainings included "admit your guilt" sessions, where white men were compelled to "confess and repent."

It's easy to see how that might leave a bad taste in people's mouths, right? Women and POC, whom these initiatives were designed to help, fared little better. They often felt as though they were being asked to speak for their entire gender or race. Others walked away believing their peers were more biased than they had initially believed. Almost everyone left the trainings unsure of the purpose or what was supposed to change.

Programs like these led to significant backlash against diversity initiatives as a whole and were frequently lampooned in the media. And when the companies that sponsored them failed to see any tangible return on their investment, many reduced those investments or even ended them completely. Ultimately, the trainings from this period did more harm than good. In many organizations, they resulted in a diversity cause setback, not advancement.

In fact, diversity trainings, are still setting the cause back. A 2016 *Harvard Business Review* article reported that mandatory trainings actually engendered ill feelings toward minorities, and formal grievance systems can even lead to a decrease in most minorities at the managerial level.[30]

Where We Are Today

After nearly a century of poor communication, unenforceable policies, and well-intentioned but ultimately shortsighted initiatives, companies are finally coming around to the idea that diverse teams really do perform better. This concept, which Kaleel Jamison realized in 1978, is even being championed by companies such as Pinterest and a raft of others.

In retrospect, it's easy to see why it took so long. Early attempts framed diversity and inclusion as a moral imperative, but those morals weren't shared by a majority of business leaders. Today, however, we've reached the point where an increasing number of decision-makers see the true value of having a diverse workforce.

For decades, "diversity" has been synonymous with unfocused and even confrontational programs that have made everyone—including POC—uneasy. So expect to see some eyes roll when you mention the "d word" at work. Prepare yourself to encounter skepticism about its efficacy. But once you're armed with the facts, you'll be able to shift the narrative and make a persuasive business case for a more diverse and inclusive workplace.

Building a Business Case for Diversity

When dealing with a topic like workplace diversity, the best approach is to stick to facts and let the statistics speak for themselves. That goes for everyone, no matter if you're in upper management or just joining a company right out of school. While more experienced professionals will likely have more opportunities to speak to the business benefits of diversity, more junior professionals should still have an informed point of view on the matter and the ability to address it with statistics when the topic comes up. And since much has been written in recent years about the impact a diverse workforce can have on financial performance, innovation, and productivity, we're fortunate to have a wealth of statistics from trusted sources.

That said, it's still important to be mindful about how, where, and even when you discuss the case for diversity. As the cofounder of a company whose business is diversity, I've had the opportunity to learn a great deal about how audiences of all ethnicities react to the topic. Some audiences that I expected to be resistant to my points have surprised me by being receptive to my message, sometimes even exceptionally so. Others, who I assumed would listen and nod their heads as they recalled their own experiences, turned out to be some of the most skeptical audiences I've encountered. Much of what I've learned, I've learned the hard way, and I hope what follows can help you avoid making the same missteps I did.

Stick to the Facts

Overcoming the long-standing skepticism toward diversity may not be easy, but it'll be almost impossible if you aren't armed with the facts. Having a more diverse workforce has a demonstrable impact on a business's performance, and you need to be able to prove it. Fortunately, we have the data to help you do just that.

Multiple studies and surveys have made it clear that diversity provides measurable gains in three key business areas: financial performance, ability to hire, and customer acquisition and retention. Let's start at the top.

FINANCIAL PERFORMANCE

Yes, companies with a more diverse workforce really do perform better. Consulting giant McKinsey & Company has found a direct correlation between racial and ethnic diversity and financial performance. According to a recent study, companies in the top quartile for racial and ethnic diversity are 35% more likely to financially outperform their less diverse competitors.[31]

That same study also found that "for every 10% increase in racial and ethnic diversity on the senior-executive team, earnings before interest and taxes (EBIT) rise 0.8%."[32] Think about that for a second: if a company makes $100 million in revenue annually, adding a single person of color to its C-suite can result in an additional $800,000 annually.

Another study, this time in the journal of the American Sociological Association (ASA), found that "the mean revenues of organizations with low levels of racial diversity are roughly $52.3 million, compared with $323.9 million for organizations with medium levels, and $808.9 million for those with high levels of diversity."[33]

The ASA study also uncovered direct correlations between workforce diversity and both profitability and market share. Just over 61% of companies with high amounts of employee diversity reported higher-than-average market share compared to just 46% of less diverse companies. When it comes to profitability, that ratio is largely the same: 61.3% of very diverse companies have higher-than-average profitability, while only 47% of homogenous companies can say the same.

There are many reasons for this, and most are directly tied to the second and third of those key business areas.

ABILITY TO HIRE

Companies today face a talent shortage of unprecedented proportions. The number of newly created jobs has outpaced the number of new hires almost every month since 2015, and the unemployment rate is at a record low. Meanwhile, the average time it takes to fill a white-collar job is now approximately sixty-eight days, twenty-six days longer than it was at the end of the last decade. And PricewaterhouseCoopers International Limited's 17th Annual Global CEO Survey discovered that 93% of CEOs "recognize the need to make a change, or are already changing their strategy for attracting and retaining talent."[34]

Those CEOs should think long and hard about implementing diversity hiring initiatives for a few very good—and very real—reasons.

By 2030, a majority of young workers will be diverse, and by 2040, will make up the majority of the U.S. population.[35] Considering that the U.S. population was 80% white as recently as the 1980s, this is a massive demographic shift. And as the population changes, so must the ways in which companies hire.

The ways in which companies have reached white professionals often don't work for attracting POC, and companies that refuse to innovate are faced with a shrinking talent pool, which leads to higher hiring costs, lengthy hiring processes, and even bad hires. Each bad hire can cost a company up to $240,000, so getting the right talent is critical.[36]

CUSTOMER ACQUISITION AND RETENTION

Given the evolving demographic statistics, understanding that diversity affects customer acquisition and retention should be a no-brainer, but when you're making a case for diversity hiring, it's critical to provide all the facts.

The majority of young workers will be diverse by 2030, and that change will result in huge growth in POC's buying power. The buying power of Black and Latinx and Hispanic people has risen dramatically in the last two decades, and it's been estimated that by 2018, the buying power of Black people will be $1.3 trillion, while that of the Latinx and Hispanic community will be $1.6 trillion. Additionally, Hispanics are expected to account for more than 55% of first-time homeowners by 2020.[37]

For business-to-consumer companies, these changes represent a seismic shift in customer base. Virtually everything we know about consumer marketing comes from a century of marketing to white people and households, meaning that companies will have to rethink their sales, marketing, and branding efforts in very short order.

Consider Dove's ill-advised Facebook ad, which seemed to feature a Black woman turning white after using Dove face wash, leading many to take offense at the implication that the Black woman was "dirty" and the white one "clean." Clearly, the company didn't test the campaign with a diverse focus group, and it's unlikely that enough empowered POC had the opportunity to review it internally.

The resulting outcry on social media was so overwhelming and immediate that within days, Dove had taken down the ad and apologized. Even so, the damage to the brand's reputation was severe. Imagine how severe that damage—and the resulting loss of revenue—would have been in a market where the majority of shoppers were POC.

But we won't have to wait until 2030 to witness the effects of shifting demographics on customer acquisition. The study documented in the ASA journal revealed that workforce diversity already has a huge impact on companies' ability to attract new customers:

> *[T]he average number of customers for organizations with low levels of racial diversity is 23,100. This compares with 587,000 for organizations with medium levels of racial diversity.*[38]

That study also demonstrated conclusively that, when it comes to customer acquisition, "The relationship between racial diversity and number of customers . . . is stronger than the impact of company size, establishment size, and organization age. . . . These results again suggest that diversity is among the most important predictors of number of customers."[39]

If a company wants to reach and engage us, it must understand us. And to understand us, companies must hire us. It's that simple.

PUT IT ALL TOGETHER: YOUR ELEVATOR PITCH FOR DIVERSITY

Statistics are crucial for building a persuasive business case for a diversity hiring program, but they're also a mouthful to recite and tough to recall. If you find yourself in a casual conversation with a colleague who expresses skepticism, keep your response factual and dispassionate, replying with language like this: "Companies with highly diverse workforces are statistically proven to outperform their competitors in total revenue, customer acquisition and retention, and market share." Then you can refer them to Jopwell.com to see the stats as an easy-to-understand infographic. Let them discover the facts for themselves; they're more likely to embrace the information they've found on their own.

THE MESSAGE SHOULD BE CLEAR FROM THE START

As we saw earlier in this chapter, diversity and inclusion is a sore subject for many, but it's also one that can have many meanings. Thanks to years of well-intentioned but flawed programs, there's been a great deal of confusion about this topic. A "diversity and inclusion program" is a broad term that can mean inclusion training, sensitivity seminars, or an initiative focused on building a more diverse workforce.

When you make the business case for diversity, it's important to use precise messaging. Specific subject lines for meeting invites, such as "Making a plan to build a more diverse team," are more likely to be well received than "Discussing a possible diversity program" because the term "diversity program" can mean many things. Lack of specificity leaves the meaning open for personal interpretation and thus risks turning off the audience at the onset.

This focus on a carefully defined message should apply to every conversation and communication concerning diversity. This is especially true when management addresses the target audience. They must make it clear that they aren't advocating discrimination against groups that fall outside their definition of diversity and that their program is exclusively focused on diversifying the company's workforce as a means to improve business performance. Empathy matters.

Imagine what a majority-group person may think when the concept of a diversity hiring program comes up. That internal dialogue might be *They're explicitly saying they want to hire someone who's not like me.* In fact, studies have shown that white men, even those who openly support diversity and inclusion, can feel threatened and undervalued by discussion of the topic.

One study put two groups of white men through a simulated hiring process at a fictional tech company. One group received recruitment materials that briefly mentioned the company's pro-diversity values; the other did not. All other information was the same for both groups. Both groups were then interviewed individually, while being filmed and having their cardiovascular responses measured.

The study found that the men who had received pro-diversity materials expected to be treated unfairly and even discriminated against. They also performed more poorly during the interviews themselves, and their cardiovascular responses showed they were more stressed than the other group. The *Harvard Business Review* nicely sums up what this means: "Importantly, diversity messages led to these effects regardless of these men's political ideology, attitudes toward minority groups, beliefs about the prevalence of discrimination against whites, or beliefs about the fairness of the world. This suggests just how widespread negative responses to diversity may be among white men: the responses exist even among those who endorse the tenets of diversity and inclusion."[40]

This is precisely why, when you're the one arguing for the value of a diverse workforce, it's critical to keep your message focused and positive. Anticipate how your audience may feel toward the topic and tailor your message accordingly. Finally, it's important to remember that making the case for diversity isn't a one-time thing. You'll need to get your message in front of the decision-makers many times, probably over the course of several months, before they start to come around. Be persistent. Be positive. Have clear takeaways from each session, and be receptive to feedback and constructive criticism.

2

THE UNSEEN OBSTACLES

The Unique Challenges People of Color Face in Today's Workplace—and How to Overcome Them

"What do you mean, you're not into basketball?"

"I just assumed you spoke Spanish."

"It's super spicy—you're into that, right?"

Without fail, every person of color has heard statements like these in their professional careers. These are widely known as "microaggressions"—subtle, often unconscious and unintentional statements or actions that express a prejudiced attitude toward members of marginalized groups. But I often use another word for them: "reminders."

These minor statements or actions serve to remind POC of our "otherness" in certain settings. They remind us that we're different from the assumed norm. They remind us that we stand out. And they remind us that, whether we like it or not, our peers pay close and special attention to everything we do and say. As a result, we experience the working world very differently from our majority-group colleagues, and we face a host of hurdles reserved for POC.

What you're about to read might make you uncomfortable. In fact, I think it *should* make any reader uncomfortable, no matter what community you belong to. These challenges should not exist, but they do. If I didn't acknowledge them, I'd be doing myself and all of you a disservice. We're going to talk about the obstacles POC continue to face in the workplace.

Understanding Implicit Bias

Every time you, I, and our cohort receive a "reminder," we need to remind ourselves where it comes from. As I mentioned, ignorance is the most likely source. But there's another source that's almost as common, and, unlike ignorance, it's much more deeply rooted and harder to dispel. I'm referring to "implicit bias"—and before we can overcome the impact of bias in others, we have to understand what it is and where it comes from.

The most thorough and accessible definition of implicit bias I've found comes from Ohio State's Kirwan Institute:

> *Implicit bias refers to the attitudes or stereotypes that affect our understanding, actions, and decisions in an unconscious manner. These biases, which encompass both favorable and unfavorable assessments, are activated involuntarily and without an individual's awareness or intentional control. Residing deep in the subconscious, these biases are different from known biases that individuals may choose to conceal for the purposes of social and/or political correctness. Rather, implicit biases are not accessible through introspection.*
>
> *The implicit associations we harbor in our subconscious cause us to have feelings and attitudes about other people based on characteristics such as race, ethnicity, age, and appearance. These associations develop over the course of a lifetime beginning*

at a very early age through exposure to direct and indirect messages. In addition to early life experiences, the media and news programming are often-cited origins of implicit associations.[41]

It's critical that we understand this definition and distinguish between implicit bias and overt racism. Overt racism is the result of conscious actions, whereas implicit bias is at the root of many of our unconscious actions. Racist attitudes can be overcome and unlearned through education and exposure, but implicit biases are difficult to diagnose and even more so to erase. We'll talk more about that in a bit, but keep it in mind as we go forward.

Another thing to keep in mind is that we all harbor countless implicit biases. They affect what we say, who our friends are, and whom we hire. Think about it like this: have you ever said something like, "Why do all guys (or girls) do X?" I know I have, and I bet you have, too. When you said this, you were giving in to an implicit bias. That's because we've unconsciously grouped a number of people together and assumed that they all exhibit the same behaviors. Now, if I asked you if you genuinely think all men or all women everywhere actually do X, your answer would be "no." You consciously know that they don't, but you've unconsciously associated an entire group with a single behavior. You aren't actively being sexist, but your implicit biases have caused you to say something sexist without your even realizing it.

Now, let's apply that lens to the modern workplace. While overt racism is relatively rare in most companies today, implicit bias is everywhere, and it has a disproportionate impact on POC.

Consider a 2003 study by economists Marianne Bertrand and Sendhil Mullainathan. In that study, they sent thousands of résumés to employers with job openings and measured which ones received callbacks and interviews. These résumés were all identical, with the exception of the name of the person applying. According to a *New York Times* article on the study, they "randomly used stereotypically

African-American names (such as 'Jamal') on some and stereotypically white names (like 'Brendan') on others."[42]

They found that résumés with stereotypically white names received roughly 50% more callbacks than those with stereotypically Black names. Again, the content of the résumés—the person's skills and experience—was identical. The only difference was the names themselves, meaning the recruiters reading them were actively screening out applicants with African-American-sounding names. But when the study was released, many human resources professionals told the economists they were "stunned."

According to Mullainathan: "They prized creating diversity in their companies, yet here was evidence that they were doing anything but. How was that possible?"

The answer, of course, is implicit bias. I'd hazard that few, if any, of the recruiters screening those résumés would consider themselves racist, but their implicit biases against POC likely played a role in their rejections of the résumés of those with ethnic-sounding names.

Let me be clear: I am in no way attempting to let recruiters and human resources professionals off the hook. Implicit bias is not an excuse. Even though their actions may have been unconscious, they have very real consequences. Had these applicants been actual job seekers, those who were POC would have suffered as a result of the recruiters' actions. I'm simply using this as an example of how implicit bias impacts professionals of color in the working world—and that's just during the hiring phase.

Once we're hired, implicit bias plays a slightly different role. It's no longer a barrier to entry, but it can be a barrier to advancement. That barrier may come from above, but it may also come from within us. After months or years of colliding with implicit biases and the actions that stem from them, we can become burned out and jaded. Those feelings are completely understandable—but they can also be career killers.

TEST YOURSELF: DO YOU HAVE IMPLICIT BIASES?

Hollywood's use of names, accents, and other attributes to telegraph a specific set of behaviors and attitudes is hardly limited to POC. The next time you're watching a movie or a television show, keep an eye out for this kind of stereotyping among other groups.

For example, was a Southern accent used as a way of suggesting that a character is uneducated? Did a television show use a girl's position as head cheerleader to suggest she's superficial and hateful to people who are less attractive or popular than she is?

If so, be cognizant of the effects these stereotypes have on your own internal biases. Once you're aware of them, you can begin to undo them on your own. It won't be easy, but awareness is the first step.

Let's look at some common issues that arise from implicit bias and talk about some strategies for overcoming them in the moment, as well as how to dispel these biases over time.

Cracking the Monolith

One very common example of implicit bias in the workplace is when our colleagues or managers assume that the people who make up various demographics all share certain attributes. These assumptions wrongly turn these groups into monoliths—massive, indistinct entities made up of people with homogenous tastes, interests, traits, preferences, or behaviors. The perception of these structures often results from limited exposure to POC and can be damaging or demoralizing to people with diverse backgrounds.

Here's an example: Paul's a young Ecuadorian account executive who graduated from Columbia University a few years ago. During a casual team outing, his coworker Tyler notices that Paul's wearing a Columbia T-shirt and asks if Paul's an alum. Paul says he is indeed.

"Oh, nice," Tyler says, "That's the American dream, huh?"

"Come again?" Paul asks.

"You know, coming to America, working hard, and watching your kid get an Ivy League education," Tyler responds. "Your folks must be super proud."

"My parents went to college, too," Paul answers. "In fact, my grandpa is a plastic surgeon in Boca Raton."

Tyler is attempting to bond with a coworker by learning more about him, but his assumption that Paul's family isn't well educated, simply because he is from Ecuador, is offensive.

Paul handles this interaction in exactly the right way: with grace and professionalism. It might have been tempting—and a completely fair question—to ask, "Are you assuming my parents aren't well educated?" But doing so would put Tyler on the defensive and leave him with a negative impression of the conversation that would likely lead him to avoid interacting with Paul in the future. Because Paul was patient and professional, he managed to crack the monolith Tyler had constructed—that all college-educated Ecuadorians must be the children of "hard working" immigrants.

Was Paul's approach as satisfying in the moment as shaming Tyler might have been? Probably not, but it's far more effective in the long run. As POC, we have a responsibility to build bridges with the majority if we want to increase the number of people who support our efforts to level the playing field. Patience is key.

Avoiding the "Culture Speaker" Trap

Another obstacle you'll encounter is being asked or expected to serve as the "culture speaker" for your particular race or ethnicity. This is an extension of the monolith problem, meaning that when this happens, one of your colleagues has already made certain assumptions about everyone who shares your background. You've probably already experienced it in some aspect of your life—and you may even have done it to others.

Have you ever asked a white friend something like, "Why do white people like golf so much?" If you have, you've essentially asked them to serve as a representative for every member of their gender or ethnicity. They might be able to tell you why they personally like or don't like golf, but they can't speak for the race.

In the workplace, however, the culture speaker trap usually presents itself when POC are asked to validate an assumption about one or more of the communities to which they belong. It usually goes something like this:

Julia, a Latina marketing manager at an electronics company, is participating in a kickoff for a new line of headphones. A product marketing executive presents a deck detailing the marketing strategy for next year, including tactics for targeting specific markets and demographics. A slide pops up featuring bilingual ad copy in English and Spanish. Beside it is a bulleted list labeled "Potential spokespeople for Hispanic market segment" that includes Selena Gomez and Luis Fonsi. Her colleagues seem to nod in approval, but the marketing executive pauses and looks directly at Julia.

Without even saying a word, it's clear that the executive is seeking Julia's approval of or feedback on the ad copy and the ideas for potential spokespeople. In so doing, she's also assuming that Julia is both able and willing to speak for every Hispanic.

Julia's in a difficult position, and none of the options available to her are great.

She could say: "Why are you looking at me?" While this would force the executive to reflect on the implicit bias behind her action, it could also be seen as confrontational and disrespectful, especially in the context of a meeting.

She could play along and say something like: "I think the copy's really solid, but I doubt we could land Selena." This would defuse the tension, but it wouldn't help the executive confront and understand her bias.

She could speak to her personal preferences and tell them whether *she* sees Selena as a compelling spokesperson, but again, she can't speak for every member of her community.

Julia's best option is to reframe the interaction by simply putting it back to the executive herself, asking: "What market research did we base this on?" By doing this, she's avoided a potentially risky confrontation and forced the exec to explain herself a bit. If the choices on the slide are based on actual market segmentation data, then Julia can offer an opinion on the data itself. But if the executive doesn't really have an answer, then Julia can explain that the market is made up of a number of different segments and includes many tastes and preferences. In so doing, she's offered insight, education and, ideally, has made the exec aware of her bias without conflict or escalation.

Coping with Repeat Offenders

While many situations that betray implicit bias will be one-offs that force you to think on your feet, there will be plenty of cases in which one individual repeatedly displays bias toward you or POC in general. This one's tricky, but there are ways to overcome it.

First, you have to consider whether the repeat offender is a peer or a superior. With a peer—someone at or below your level in the company's organizational structure—your approach should begin casually. If it's a superior—your manager or anyone who outranks you—you'll have to be a bit more strategic and careful. Let's go through examples of both scenarios in detail.

THE PEER

Hadley has just joined the sales team at a young startup. She graduated from Howard a few months before, and she's eager for the chance to make an impact on the business. The team is small but growing fast, and she's the only person of color on the team. She gets along well with her manager and her team members, but there have already been a few moments in her brief tenure that made her uncomfortable, and they all originated from Chris, another sales rep.

He's made several comments that reveal implicit biases about and toward POC. Some have even been intended as compliments, such as the time he praised her for being articulate and professional after overhearing her on a sales call (she's never heard him pay the same compliment to anyone else). Hadley's reasonably sure Chris has never meant to offend her or cause discomfort, but that's not important. His comments still hurt—and may even impact her engagement and job performance over time.

Hadley's talked this over with her friends a few times, and some suggested she go directly to human resources. But she's not sure that's the right choice. She genuinely wants to get along well with Chris, and she doesn't want to get him in trouble. So what should she do?

One option is casually asking Chris to grab a coffee. Once they're away from the office and in a neutral setting, she can tell Chris that some of his comments have made her uncomfortable and explain why his actions bothered her and how they made her feel. In my experience, most people are genuinely apologetic and even shocked that what they said or did caused offense (these biases are implicit, after all). It's likely that Chris will react the same way. If he's receptive, Hadley can offer to privately point out future examples of bias.

If he's not, however, then she'll have to go to her manager. This, too, can be a casual conversation, but Hadley should be prepared to give specific examples of bias. She may even need to educate her manager on what implicit bias is and how it affects POC in the workplace. Her manager will likely offer to pull Chris aside and have a conversation about his behavior. If this solves the problem, great. If it doesn't, she and her manager should get human resources involved and begin documenting his actions with an eye toward disciplinary action or even termination. That's a drastic step and should be reserved as a last resort—but it's definitely on the table.

THE SUPERIOR

Almost a year later, Hadley's become a star on the sales team. The company's just hired a new vice president of product, and he's asked the leaders of each function to nominate someone from their team to serve on a "discovery team." The team, made up of client-facing employees from across sales, account management, and customer support, is designed to surface insights about what customers both enjoy and struggle with when using the company's software products. When Hadley's boss announced that she'd be representing the sales team, the VP replied: "Oh good! We'll have some diversity on the team."

While it's great that he welcomes diverse perspectives, it's not so great that he voiced that in front of everyone. It reminds Hadley of her "otherness" and reinforces the idea in the minds of her colleagues.

During the team's first meeting, her coworkers enthusiastically offer insights. Before Hadley has the chance to chime in, the VP says:

"Let's hear from someone who isn't a white dude. Hadley, what do you think?" Again, not a bad sentiment, but the VP voices it in the wrong way. He could've simply said, "Hadley, what do you think?" As the team meets each week, the VP's behavior becomes a pattern. He continually reinforces Hadley's differences, and after a few weeks, she decides something needs to be done.

Like Julia, Hadley doesn't really have an option for confronting the VP's biases during the meeting in a fashion that wouldn't be viewed as potentially combative or disrespectful. Her best option here is to seek assistance from higher up in the company's chain of command, and her first step should be talking to her manager.

She can broach the subject during their weekly one on one. She'll need to give concrete examples of what the VP said and why these statements made her feel uneasy. She should then solicit her manager's guidance on how to handle the situation. Since it's a small company, her manager may recommend she speak to the VP directly and candidly—perhaps an invitation to coffee outside the office. Were this a larger organization, however, her boss would likely offer to have that conversation with the VP herself. But no matter how large or heavily matrixed your company is, always look to your manager for guidance when confronting bias from a superior. Some company cultures encourage executives to seek feedback from junior team members, but not all. Tread carefully here.

Playing the Long Game

The examples just described are effective for confronting bias with individual coworkers in the moment, but they won't erase implicit bias in these individuals—and the rest of your organization—immediately. Eliminating biases takes time, effort, and buy-in from the biased individuals themselves, but there are some things you can do to get the ball rolling.

The first is to begin referring POC from your personal and professional networks when new roles become available. Consider this "exposure therapy." Many of our colleagues have few POC in their lives outside of work, so the more our coworkers are exposed to POC, the more likely they are to begin recognizing and overcoming the implicit biases they hold toward and about us.

The second thing you can do is offer to coordinate a series of implicit bias trainings. There are a number of consulting services available for conducting these trainings, but getting the approval for the budget to pay for them may prove difficult. If that's the case with your organization, ask an academic or industry expert if they might be willing to do a small fireside chat free of charge or for some form of nonmonetary compensation your company may be able to provide—such as a live Twitter session from the event on an active corporate Twitter account or having your company write a press release detailing the visit. Use this as a proof of concept. If it goes well, you can offer to bring in another expert for other teams or even the entire company, and if it's well attended, you might be able to secure the budget for the next presentation.

This process also creates an opportunity to be a leader and gain recognition. That's not the primary goal, of course, but it's a nice benefit. It might be uncomfortable at first—it's an uncomfortable topic, after all—but I can help you with that.

Learning to Love the Spotlight in Four (Not So) Easy Steps

Have you ever boarded a crowded train, plane, or bus and thought: *Why is everyone staring at me?*

You wonder if there's something on your face—but there's not. When you're the only person of color in the room, it's natural to feel singled out and feel as if everyone else is looking at you. It's what social psychologists call the "spotlight effect," which is the term we use for the phenomenon in which people feel as if they're being noticed more than they actually are. In truth, everyone isn't focusing on you. In fact, almost no one is truly looking at you.

If you've ever been one of a few—or the only—POC in your workplace, you've probably experienced the spotlight effect, except people *were* focusing on you and it wasn't temporary. No, I don't mean that people at work are staring at you constantly throughout the workday. I mean they are likely paying more attention to what you do and say than to the words and actions of your majority-group coworkers.

There are a few reasons for this. First, as one of a few POC in the workplace, you inherently stand out. Your physical appearance is different. Your cultural touchstones are likely different, too. But, perhaps more important, your life experiences are different, and that means you likely have a different perspective on things. When you voice your perspective, it's likely to be noticed more, simply because it's different. That certainly doesn't make it bad or wrong. But your coworkers will likely ask you more questions about it simply because it's new to them, and that can feel like they disagree or don't understand even when they're just genuinely curious.

Another reason the things you do and say will receive more attention is—you guessed it—because your colleagues' implicit biases mean they have certain expectations about you and your abilities. Some will have never encountered a person of color in your field before, so they may assume that you're some brilliant unicorn. These people may have uninformed expectations about what you can do. An unfortunate few, on the other hand, will think that you might have been hired to satisfy a diversity quota, and therefore they expect your work to be subpar. They'll try to pick your work apart looking for flaws in support of that expectation. Whatever the case may be, it's a simple fact that your work will likely receive more attention than that of your colleagues.

What we experience in these very real conditions is quite similar to what we think is happening when we experience the spotlight effect. Our minds aren't playing tricks on us here—we *are* actually in the spotlight. It can be burdensome and taxing, but only if we let it.

STEP 1 CHANGE YOUR VIEW

A few years into my career, I was texting with a friend about my growing frustration with being in the spotlight. I felt as if I had to be "on" all the time. I felt as if any mistake I made would be magnified a thousand fold, while the rest of my colleagues might be forgiven more easily. If you're a person of color, you've probably had this same conversation countless times.

My friend graciously let me vent for a bit. Then he sent me this quote: "If you are caught unprepared by a sudden rainstorm, you should not run foolishly down the road or hide under the eaves of houses. You are going to get soaked either way. Accept that from the beginning, and go on your way. This way, you will not be distressed by a little rain. Apply this lesson to everything."

That internet-popular quote turned out to be from the writings of a seventeenth-century samurai named Yamamoto Tsunetomo, and it's radically changed how I view the spotlight.

In simplest terms, Yamamoto's analogy reminds us that, in some situations, nothing we do will change the outcome. Now, let's apply that wisdom to the spotlight. First, accept that the attention POC receive in the workplace is the norm for now, and that's unlikely to end any time soon. This will decrease as demographics shift in the United States, but that's more than a decade away from happening.

Next, understand that, while the spotlight may make us uncomfortable, it's not necessarily a harmful thing. As long as you conduct yourself in a professional manner and the work you do is effective and impactful, the spotlight can't harm you. But that's easier said than done.

STEP 2 UP YOUR GAME

The old adage that POC have to work twice as hard for half the respect is as true today as it was decades ago, so your performance has to be exemplary, and your reputation must be beyond reproach.

Wait—isn't this unfair? Yes, it's very unfair, and anyone who tells you otherwise is either in denial or lying to you. We can and should work to dismantle this double standard. But at the same time, we have careers to build, and that means we also have to play within the existing rules of the game, no matter how unfair they may be. In this case, that means bringing your A game every single day and continuously delivering work that exceeds your manager's expectations and outshines the output of your peers.

Think about it like this: if you're a person of color in a nondiverse workforce, your colleagues may receive far less attention than you do. The same is true for their work. You, however, may not ever get a pass. Everything you do may be magnified, and it had better hold up to the greater scrutiny it will most likely receive. As a result, you have to hold yourself to a higher standard.

If you're preparing a presentation to give tomorrow and it's not 100% on point, you're going to have to cancel those plans with your friends. If you're calling on a client tomorrow morning and your pitch deck isn't airtight, that date is going to have to wait. Getting ahead in the spotlight means putting in more hours, more work, and more sweat. If you want to be successful, this is your new normal.

And yes, there will be times when you get jaded. Burned out. Resentful. No one could blame you. But every time these negative emotions appear, balance them by reminding yourself that there's an endgame here. You're investing in your future, and that requires sacrifice and discipline. Instead of trying to avoid having your work examined closely, you're embracing it.

You might not see the payoff tomorrow, but you'll see it soon enough.

STEP 3 MAKE IT WORK

Now that you've accepted the situation and adapted your attitude toward work accordingly, it's time to make the spotlight work for you.

I know from experience that the spotlight can be a burden, but it can also be a blessing. Sure, POC get a lot of unwanted attention—but think of how many of our colleagues would crave that attention. In a somewhat perverse sense, we've been given a gift—you're being seen!—and it's up to us to use it wisely and strategically.

If you've been holding yourself to a higher standard and are confident that your work is exceptional, don't sit back and treat the attention your work receives as a burden. Revel in it. Use it. Instead of feeling embarrassed, ashamed, or anxious that your work is getting noticed, treat it as an opportunity to showcase what you can do. Remember, your colleagues might be dying for the same kind of attention, so don't take it for granted. Every minute your boss spends examining your work is a chance to demonstrate your ability to add value for the business.

I'd even challenge you to take it a step further and seek *more* attention. When a special project comes along, raise your hand. Volunteer to work on a team or a task force or offer to lead an initiative. As long as it won't impact the quality of your core work—and as long as your boss signs off on it—volunteering to take on additional responsibilities can be a fast path to promotion. If nothing else, it can expose you to other senior stakeholders in the organization and elevate your profile.

In a nutshell, if you're going to be in the spotlight, you might as well get something out of it.

STEP 4 STAY FOCUSED

I know from experience that doing what I've just described is anything but easy. It's a constant struggle, but persistence pays off.

Affirmations and visualization help here. Every morning before work, say the following aloud to yourself:

- I'm letting my colleagues see me, and that's good for me—and my career.
- If I do exceptional work and build strong relationships with my managers and teammates, the spotlight will help me, not harm me.
- The attention I receive is an opportunity to improve myself and add value for my employer, but it's up to me to make that happen.
- I hold myself and my work to the highest possible standard. "Good enough" is never good enough for me.

This won't sink in after just one day, so commit to making it a practice. Set an alert on your phone that reminds you to focus on these four simple statements for a few minutes at the same time each day. This will help you not only internalize the wisdom that the spotlight can't hurt you, but also be more forgiving of and understanding toward your coworkers. After all, you can't do your best work and be your best self if you resent the people with whom you share an office.

If you're skeptical, I don't blame you. I get that it's hard to come to grips with this, especially when you spend each day under a microscope. But I urge you to try it for a month. As soon as I was able to truly take these concepts to heart, I was far less bothered by the spotlight. It even helped me learn that I could use the spotlight to contribute to the business and advance my career. I'm confident it'll do the same for you.

Why Employers Should Be Invested in Addressing These Obstacles

It bears repeating: Business leaders also should be removing these obstacles, not only because it's the right thing to do but it also affects their bottom line in the form of employee retention. When we talk about employee retention, we're talking about the rate at which existing employees leave a company voluntarily. The reasons they leave vary widely: some may leave for another job that pays more, offers more responsibility, or provides a chance to learn new skills. Others, however, may leave for less positive reasons, like burnout, being passed over for a promotion, or frustration with the company culture.

For an employer, a poor retention rate is costly. They'll have to recruit, interview, hire, and train the departing employee's replacement, all of which require substantial time and money. Then they have to give the new hire time to get up to speed, which means a period of lower productivity that can last from a few weeks to several months, depending on the complexity of the role. During this period, it's common for team members to pick up a new hire's slack, which can lead to late nights, heavy workloads, and high stress—all of which can lead to still more turnover.

The average total cost for replacing an employee is roughly 20% of that employee's annual salary.[43] If a startup loses an experienced mobile developer, for example, and that developer was making $150,000 a year, it'll cost the company $30,000 to replace her—and that's just for a single employee. If that same company has a 13% voluntary turnover rate—about the national average for all industries, and a number that's likely to climb as the economy continues to improve—they could spend hundreds of thousands of dollars every year just to replace departing talent.[44]

Some turnover is, of course, normal and should be expected. But when a company experiences high rates of employee turnover, it's likely a sign that something is very wrong with their corporate culture and values. Maybe the company's leadership fails to communicate their vision and goals effectively. Maybe their culture is beginning to turn a little toxic. Maybe they're just not paying competitive rates.

Whatever the reasons, companies often take the same steps to address them. Exit interviews will probably be implemented. Someone will commission a competitive analysis of salary offerings around the industry. A "culture committee" will probably be founded. Make no mistake: these are all good actions and smart decisions. But they don't go far enough. That's because companies often focus exclusively on *why* they're losing talent—and little (or not at all) on *who* they're losing.

If I pulled the names of twenty random companies out of a hat and asked them to show me a demographic breakdown of employees who voluntarily left in 2017, I'm willing to bet that at least half of those reports would indicate disproportionately higher turnover among POC.

A 2017 study by the Kapor Center for Social Impact, a research organization dedicated to improving diversity in the technology ecosystem and making entrepreneurship more diverse and inclusive, found a direct correlation between levels of workforce diversity and the treatment of diverse employees and employee retention. Their 2017 Tech Leavers Study polled two thousand American professionals who had left a job in tech within the last three years and found that:

- Nearly 40% of respondents indicated that unfairness or mistreatment played a significant role in their decision to leave their company. The most likely group to leave due to unfairness was underrepresented men.

- Men and women of color experienced stereotyping at twice the rate of white and Asian men and women.
- 30% of underrepresented women of color were passed over for promotion.[45]

These statistics should be sobering for any business leader in tech. But the study also offered some key actions that leadership can take to prevent turnover among underrepresented groups.

Almost two-thirds of tech job leavers indicated that they would have stayed if their employer had taken steps to fix company culture. Having a diversity and inclusion strategy was associated with fewer reports of unfairness, bullying, and stereotyping, and lower rates of employees leaving due to unfairness. Additionally, having a comprehensive diversity and inclusion strategy had a much greater impact on retention than individual initiatives (such as implicit bias training).[46]

In short, greater diversity has a measurable impact on employee retention, and there are actionable steps that executives can take to remove obstacles, reduce stereotyping, and create more inclusive workplaces. It's not just a nice thing to do—it'll save a company hundreds of thousands, or even millions, of dollars.

Now that we've articulated the challenges POC face at work and how to overcome the most common varieties, let's shift gears and talk about how every professional can add value and be a high performer in the spotlight at work.

A CALL TO ACTION

3

BEING AN ATHLETE AT WORK

What Sports Can Teach Us about Accountability, Relationships, and Goal Setting

Up until now, we've been talking about the state of diversity in the workforce and what professionals of color often experience at work. In this section, we're going to shift gears and discuss strategies that entry- and mid-level professionals of all backgrounds can use to add value at work, build relationships, and grow their careers.

But first, let me tell you about the time I met Magic Johnson.

A few years ago, Jopwell was raising a round of funding, and my cofounder, Ryan Williams, and I were taking meetings with a variety of potential investors. One day, we found ourselves in a New York City hotel waiting to meet with NBA Hall of Famer, entrepreneur, and investor Earvin "Magic" Johnson, Jr. In case you're not a basketball fan or maybe just too young to remember, he's kind of a huge deal. He won five NBA championships and three league most valuable player awards during his thirteen-year career with the Los Angeles Lakers, not to mention a gold medal from the 1992 Olympics.

Following basketball, he became an accomplished entrepreneur. For a lifelong basketball fan and burgeoning entrepreneur myself, meeting him was like a dream come true.

Like countless other die-hard basketball fans, I'd spent hours as a kid watching Mr. Johnson play, all the while daydreaming about having the ball while the clock ticks away. At the last second, I—as he so often did—would drain a game-winning fade-away jumper. Now I was actually going to meet one of my childhood heroes. I still remember what went through my head when he opened the door:

He is so much taller than I thought.
This is actually Magic Johnson. I'm meeting with Magic Johnson.
Am I dressed appropriately?
What do I call him? "Magic?" "Earvin?" "Mr. Johnson?"

The meeting began with Ryan and me explaining our backgrounds and why we had started Jopwell. We spoke about our upbringing, the time we'd spent in finance, the barriers we had experienced being recruited as two African-American males, and the need that Jopwell serves.

We also went into detail about the previous year—growing the business, hiring employees, building the brand, raising money, and partnering with amazing companies. We got into the nitty-gritty of the business, explaining how we make money, how user growth works, and our employees' backgrounds. At no point in the conversation did he ever ask why Jopwell was important. He already knew.

After chatting for about forty-five minutes, Mr. Johnson asked me a question that no other investor had ever asked us before. It was simple, but it sparked a conversation that I'll always remember and cherish.

"What's been the biggest obstacle or barrier that you've had to personally overcome?"

My answer came instantly: "I've been an athlete all my life," I said. "I was always the stand-out athlete in my circle of friends and at school. It was who I was. It was how I identified myself. I played basketball in college and enjoyed a successful career. I was a three-year starter, played on several nationally televised games, and enjoyed all the fruits that came with being an athlete on a college campus.

"However," I continued, "during my freshman-year Christmas break, while at a party in my neighborhood, an older neighbor asked me what school I went to. I told him Yale. His next question was, without any hesitation, 'What sport do you play?'

"I was taken aback, angry that because I was a young Black Yale student, he assumed I had to play a sport to attend the school. So from that point on, whenever anyone asked if I played a sport, I told them I didn't. I wanted them to see my intelligence and my other accomplishments. I didn't want people thinking I was *only* an athlete."

Mr. Johnson listened intently and nodded along.

I went on to explain that after graduation, I'd had a really difficult time adjusting to life outside of sports. I'd spent my entire life working to be the best athlete I could be. And then, all of a sudden, I was ashamed to identify as one. Even worse, I didn't know how else to identify myself. That changed when I started Jopwell. I now identify as an entrepreneur, but even that is a new concept to me. It's an identity that I still work at managing.

Now Mr. Johnson was smiling. Little did I know that what he was about to say would help reshape my perception of myself and how I viewed the world.

He started by explaining how his entire life people had identified him as "Magic" Johnson, and not Earvin Johnson. Everyone knew him as the athlete before they knew the whole person. Being one of the best basketball players of all time, living in Los Angeles during the tumultuous eighties and nineties, and being an international celebrity, he had had to accept that the world viewed and knew him as Magic.

Following his time in the NBA, he wanted to do more. He knew he had the background to be as successful off the court as he was on the court. He'd always wanted to be a businessman, even in college, so he applied his experience growing up in the hardworking town of Lansing, Michigan, his fame as a basketball player, and the values he had learned during his career—discipline, adaptability, hard work, confidence, competitiveness, and teamwork.

Those character traits allowed him to carve out space in the crowded business landscape of Los Angeles and eventually to become the mogul he is today. He knew there were plenty of great businessmen and women, but he had the confidence to realize that none of them could bring what he could bring to the table.

This eventually led to a highly successful partnership with Starbucks. Mr. Johnson explained that through research he conducted in the late nineties, he learned that most Starbucks stores experience peak sales before noon. Once the afternoon hit—especially in suburban towns, where Starbucks were almost exclusively located at the time—virtually no one was purchasing coffee.

With Mr. Johnson's intimate understanding of urban America, he saw an opportunity not only to develop Starbucks in new communities but also to drive afternoon and evening sales. He presented a proposal to Starbucks' senior leadership detailing his plan for franchising in urban communities, despite the fact that Starbucks did not allow franchises. He identified robust areas for store placement, leveraged relationships with local community-based organizations for hiring, and designed an environment where people could gather for meetings, to socialize, or both. In 1998, the senior leadership team decided to take a chance on his plan and allowed him to open or purchase more than a hundred franchises in urban communities.

Starbucks also allowed him to adjust the menu and add picnic tables outside to provide a welcoming atmosphere for chess and card players. Those key elements made his stores local favorites, allowing him to sell more coffee and food items. In 2010, he sold his franchises back to Starbucks and cashed in around $70 million through the divestment.

By the time Mr. Johnson finished his story, I no longer felt the need to continue hiding my own past as an athlete. After all, that experience had given me the discipline, drive, leadership, and team-oriented mentality I needed to excel professionally. Hearing his story also made me realize that each of us has our own unique gifts and talents, and we can apply those abilities to deliver value at work and grow our careers. Now let's look at ways we can apply that lesson every day.

How to Use the Athlete's Mindset to Add Value

In the sports world, success can seem deceptively simple: build a team of the most talented athletes available, score more points than the other team, and win the game. Do that again and again until you've won the championship. Easy, right?

I can see how you might think this way, especially if you've never played on a disciplined, well-coached team. If you have, you'll understand that, while winning is the ultimate goal, every game is a complex ballet in which each team member has distinct responsibilities and goals and adds value in different ways.

When everyone involved knows the playbook and understands how and where to contribute, wins come easily. If, on the other hand, each player tries to score every time they have the ball, the game ends up a confused mess. This team will almost certainly lose again and again, and the locker-room culture will soon become tense and toxic. The same is true at work—each team member has a playbook to follow and a role to play according to their skills and abilities; each offers unique ways to contribute to successful business outcomes.

Now, let's use this framework to discuss the ways every young professional can excel at work, make a positive impact for their employers, and grow their career.

Understanding and Exceeding What's Expected of You

During my basketball career, I was always the point guard. In that role, my responsibilities were clear: understand my coach's game plan and run the offense accordingly, create opportunities for my teammates and myself, and control the pace of play while my team was on offense. As such, I was judged primarily on my ability to create assists (passes to my teammates that led to baskets) and minimize turnovers.

A center's responsibilities, on the other hand, are much different. As the largest players on the court, they're tasked with guarding the low post, pulling down rebounds, and blocking shots—a very different set of duties from those I had while running point. The same is true for the remaining three players on the floor. To win, each player has to stick to their role and execute to the best of their ability. Playing your current position at work is no different.

The first step toward adding value is understanding exactly what's expected of you and how those expectations influence business outcomes. In other words, what is your role, and why does it matter? You might be thinking: *I know what my job is. Why are you telling me this?* I'm making this point because I've often seen young professionals who know what their role is but not why it matters within the organization. As a result, they struggle to make meaningful contributions and get ahead. To help you avoid this trap, I've created the "what, why, how, and where" method.

Let's say, for example, you work in account management for a business-to-business (b2b) software company. Your biggest responsibility is keeping your company's customers happy. That may mean answering their questions or solving problems they encounter with your product or service. But the reason you're performing these tasks—and the reason your role exists in the first place—is to help your company retain those customers, create opportunities to sell them new products, or expand the relationship to new divisions within the customers' businesses.

In this example, we have clear answers to the four "what, why, how, and where" questions:

What is my job? Keeping my customers happy and engaged.

Why does my role exist? To retain our customers and preserve revenue.

How does my manager judge my performance? Customer retention and the amount of money clients spend with us.

Where can I add value beyond my day-to-day responsibilities? By creating or identifying opportunities for account growth.

Take a few minutes to answer these four questions for yourself. I strongly recommend writing them out on a sheet of paper or in a journal, rather than on your computer or other device. Getting away from screens and the distractions that come with them is very helpful for strategic thinking.

You should be able to answer the first three questions with relative ease, but the fourth can often be tricky. Determining where you can add value outside of your daily routine requires you to truly understand the needs of your business—and how to overdeliver without sacrificing performance. If you're unsure about this one, it's a great talking point for your next one-on-one with your manager.

Broach the subject by saying something like: "I'd like to be sure my work has maximum impact on the business's overall goals. What can I do in addition to my daily responsibilities to add value and help you exceed your own goals?"

The reason for framing the subject this way is simple. Your manager is responsible for your and your team's performance. If you underdeliver, your manager is going to hear about it from his or her manager. If you overdeliver, your manager gets to report your successes up the chain of command and will reap the benefits accordingly. And since your manager has the most impact on your ability to get promoted and develop as a professional, adding unexpected value that enables her to shine is a direct investment in your career growth. In short, when she looks good, you benefit.

Your manager should be able to answer this question easily. After all, she is probably swamped and will likely welcome additional effort. If so, make sure you walk away with a clear understanding of what's needed, as well as what success looks like. If your manager tells you that she'd love it if you could put together a training session for your team on how to identify opportunities for account growth, be sure you know when she expects to have it, what the desired outcomes are, and what format she expects it to take. Always ask; never assume (within reason). Assumptions often result in wasted work and disappointment, neither of which adds value.

But—and this is key—before you have this conversation, be sure that you're delivering against expectations consistently and effectively. Overdelivering requires time and energy, and you can't spare either of those if you're not already fulfilling the basics of your role. If this is the case, don't stress out or feel guilty. Instead, detail what you need to do to meet the current expectations and start there. If you identify another way you're motivated to add value, you'll have that contribution to work toward.

The most important goals, no matter what your current performance is like, are creating close relationships with your manager and others, getting some help from a mentor, developing a feedback system with your peers, and—finally—making your plan for adding value. These will create a clear path to success and serve as a model for evaluating and improving your performance over time.

Build a Successful Relationship with Your Manager

In basketball, your coach controls your destiny. They decide how much playing time you'll get, what position you'll play, and even if you're going to make the team. They also determine when and how much you practice, as well as which of your skills needs improvement. That's why building a productive, successful relationship with your coach is key. If you don't, you're going to be riding the bench for the season—and that's if you manage to stay on the team.

I was especially fortunate to have great coaches. They gave me expert guidance that made me a better player and teammate, and their belief in me gave me the confidence I needed to excel. But that wouldn't have happened if I hadn't worked hard to earn their trust. I wanted my coaches to trust me with the ball when the game was on the line, so I knew I had to make sure they had faith in my ability to run the offense effectively and give my teammates opportunities to reach their potential. They also had to know that I was playing not for personal glory, but with the best interests of the team—and even the entire program—in mind.

That kind of relationship doesn't form overnight. It takes patience, persistence, and hard work. It's not easy, but if you want to do your best work, get promoted, and build a powerful professional brand, it's definitely not optional. Your manager is the most important decision-maker when it comes to these objectives. You have to have him or her in your corner if you're going to win. To ensure that, you need to build a relationship that's founded on four key elements:

- Open, frequent communication
- Accountability
- Visible investment
- Mutual trust

OPEN, FREQUENT COMMUNICATION

This is the fulcrum on which every other aspect of your relationship pivots. Open and frequent communication is absolutely critical to building this relationship—and so is honesty. Being honest with your manager is easy when sharing a win but much more difficult when you're struggling. After all, admitting that you need support or have made a mistake means making yourself vulnerable to criticism and judgment. But allowing yourself to be vulnerable and admitting you need some help is the first step on the road to improvement.

If you don't already have a regularly scheduled one-on-one session with your manager, ask to set one up. Explain to them that greater access to their guidance and insight will help you do your job more effectively. If you have these sessions on the calendar already, then be sure you're using them as effectively as possible. This can be some of the most valuable time you'll spend at work, so be sure you enter every session with a structured agenda that contains at least four items:

- A win you've experienced over the previous week
- A problem you encountered and how you solved it
- A challenge that you'd like some guidance on
- A request for feedback from your manager on your performance

The first two points allow you to demonstrate success, autonomy, and problem-solving skills. The last two tell your manager that you're being open and honest about the problems you're facing and that you're interested in their feedback and dedicated to improving. Write down their feedback, and send them an email after the meeting that recaps your discussion on each point. This will help track your progress as you grow and develop, and it provides a record of their constructive criticism you can reference in the weeks to come. In each subsequent one-on-one, provide updates on what you're doing to address their feedback.

Don't limit your communication to one-on-ones, of course. Be responsive to emails and messaging apps, and ask for help in the moment when you need it. Sure, this is good manners, but it's also another way of demonstrating commitment.

ACCOUNTABILITY

Do what you say you're going to do.

This seems obvious for professionals who want to get ahead, but it's also one of the most difficult objectives to fulfill. Because you're ambitious, you want to dazzle your manager and your peers by over-delivering. But no matter how hard you work, you'll inevitably come up short at one point or another. A stakeholder in a project will be late with a deliverable, or life will just get in the way. When this happens, it can be hard to own your mistakes and admit to your manager that you failed, even when the error was minor.

Most managers are understanding and forgiving when you miss a goal or a deliverable. As long as you made your best effort, admit your mistake, and have a plan for avoiding it in the future, your boss won't lose nearly as much confidence in you as he or she will if you try to dodge guilt or point the finger at someone else.

A major component of accountability is honesty with yourself about your time and your abilities. When your manager asks you to prepare a thirty-slide deck and wants an ETA, your first instinct may be to say "Tomorrow!" Instead, stop and consider this project in the context of all your other work. Be realistic about a delivery date. A good manager will appreciate a thoughtful response, so ask yourself the following:

- How long will this project take me?
- Do I have all the information I need to complete this task? If not, do I know where to get that information or whom to ask?
- If I do know whom to ask, how sure am I that they'll get back to me in a timely fashion?

The answers here should dictate how soon and how well can you complete the task. To be doubly sure you've set realistic expectations, multiply how long you think it will take you by two. Trust me—things always come up.

Another approach to building a reputation for accountability is adapting an ownership mindset. If you're the person in charge of a deliverable, you're responsible for the success of all of its pieces, as well as its timely delivery. If it's a group effort and a coworker fails to deliver on their part of the work, don't point the finger or try to throw them under the bus. Accept that you're the "face" of the project and your manager holds you accountable. Ultimately, you're the one who didn't deliver, so be prepared to accept criticism when a project goes wrong.

I learned this lesson early in my basketball career. If a teammate missed a pass and the coach took me to task for it, I found out pretty quickly that blaming my teammate for being in the wrong place or not being aware of the play didn't hold much water. I was running the offense, and if something went wrong, I had to carry that weight. Being able to do this is a sign of maturity and leadership.

Accepting criticism, however, is not the same thing as hanging your head and taking the blame. Instead, offer your manager a blameless explanation of how and where the project fell short and detail the steps you'll take to ensure that it doesn't happen again.

VISIBLE INVESTMENT

If your manager feels as if you're clocking in and checking out, you're not likely to earn recognition or a promotion. Exceptional performance goes a long way toward showing investment, but if you don't engage with your coworkers and participate in group projects or cross-functional teams, the message you're sending is that you're showing up to do only what's asked of you and to collect a paycheck. Your manager needs to feel as if you're invested in the mission.

This can be tricky, especially since many of us grew up hearing that if we show up on time, keep our heads down, and work hard, success will come our way. Don't get me wrong—hard work and punctuality still matter a great deal, but they're only two pieces of the puzzle. In today's collaborative, open-office environments, optics matter more than ever.

Do you spend your workday with headphones on? Do you avoid attending optional meetings or training sessions? Do you prefer to eat lunch at your desk while your colleagues gather on couches and chat for a bit? If so, you might be sending the wrong message to your manager and others. Not that there's anything wrong with that way of working. There will be times when you're on deadline and need to hunker down and get work done. But if that's your default mode every day, you're not telling your manager and peers that you're invested in the team's success, nor are you demonstrating leadership potential.

This may seem a bit paradoxical. After all, shouldn't focusing on your work signal your commitment to the business? Well, yes—in theory. However, it's more likely to signal that you're invested only in getting your own work done and that you have little to no interest in the bigger picture. Instead, you need to balance your focus between your own work and your team's overall goals.

This a tightrope walk that's hard to master, but with a little practice and a lot of mindfulness, you can get there.

If I had showed up to basketball practice every day, did what I was told to do—even if I did it exceptionally well—and then packed my gear and left without a word when practice was over, what do you think my coaches would've made of it? Would they have thought I had the leadership skills needed to play my position? Would they have thought I was interested in winning? I doubt it. They might have thought I had talent, but they certainly wouldn't have handed me the keys to the offense.

To demonstrate my desire to lead, I had to show up early, stay late, and engage with my teammates before, during, and after practice. I had to encourage them to get better and go above and beyond. How well I played was only part of the equation—and that's true for you, too.

Be mindful of the vibe you give off around the office. Even if you're swamped, take time away from your desk and get lunch or a coffee with colleagues. Join task forces or cross-functional teams, even if that means you need to stay an hour later after work to catch up. Offer to take on special projects or lead initiatives, and make sure your manager is aware that you're doing it. I'm not suggesting you put on a show or be someone you're not; I'm simply saying that optics matter, and you can't get ahead if your contributions go unnoticed.

MUTUAL TRUST

The three variables we've discussed so far contribute to one of the most critical aspects of a successful manager-employee relationship: shared trust. Ideally, your manager should trust you to execute from

Day One, but it's up to you to maintain that trust through communication, investment, and accountability. If you want the ball when the game's on the line, you have to demonstrate these traits continuously. But that's not all; there are still a few nuances to explore before we move on.

You've probably heard the old axiom that trust is a two-way street. It may seem like a cliché, but that doesn't mean it's not true. If you want your manager to trust you with the kind of responsibilities that will help you grow as a professional, you have to earn it. Focusing on the items I've outlined will get you 75% of the way there, but you'll never go all the way without first trusting your manager.

This means assuming from the outset that he or she has a vision for your team and has the best interests of you and your company at heart. This doesn't mean you can't ask questions or have doubts from time to time. But if you're skeptical of your manager's motivations or doubt their competency, you're never going to buy in to the mission, and that's going to be evident to your manager and your teammates.

If I had second-guessed my coaches' calls or constantly questioned their decisions, I would've been shown a seat on the bench. You risk the same fate, so trust your leaders, and make that trust visible. If you do—and if you demonstrate the traits we've talked about thus far—their trust in you will increase, and you'll reap the rewards.

COLLABORATE AND SOLICIT FEEDBACK

At every stage of my basketball career, my coaches always had a plan for how I could improve. When I was in elementary school, I assumed they knew best and followed their instructions—I did the drills and exercises they gave me because they told me to, not because I particularly wanted to. As I matured, I began to see all that practice paying off during games. It was making me better, which meant I had more success on the court.

And at some point during middle school, a lightbulb finally came on: practice wasn't valuable just because it made me better, but because in making me better, it made my team better, too. When I'm better, I can help others get better. And when we all get better, we win more games.

Once I made the connection between my individual efforts and the team's outcomes, a transformation happened—I started to love practice. I no longer did the drills just because my coaches told me to. I did them with a new perspective, eager to improve and help my team win. I began identifying weaknesses in my own game and worked to improve the areas that needed the most development. I also started asking for feedback from my coaches and teammates on how I could grow as a player and a leader, and they were happy to give it.

I'll admit, I wasn't really prepared for just how happy they were to give feedback or how much feedback they actually had to give. My game was good, but they made it clear to me just how much better I could become. Perhaps even more important, they held me accountable for improving in the skills we all agreed I could improve. This gave me added incentive to get better, not just to meet their expectations but to exceed them. It lit a fire in me that's still there today, and I want to light the same fire in you.

Your manager and team members count on you to bring your A game to work every day, just as my coaches and teammates expected me to give all I had on the court. They may not tell you when you're not carrying your load, but trust me—they notice. And, like my younger self, you may think you're crushing it day in and day out, but you can't know unless you ask.

So ask.

Ask your peers what you can improve. Take them out for coffee or a drink. If you don't feel comfortable doing this, create an anonymous survey. How you get this feedback doesn't matter. What matters is that you're:

- Open to receiving it in whatever form it takes.
- Able to accept it without getting defensive.
- Willing to take it to heart and act on it.
- Committed to acting on it and staying accountable for it.

If any one of these things isn't true, then you're not committed to getting better and adding value. To improve, you must be willing to listen and accept some potentially hard truths about your performance. Remember, a constructive critique is not a personal attack, so be mindful about separating criticism about your work from criticism about yourself. The two are distinct, and if you don't keep that in mind, you risk becoming resentful, and that will only drag you down. You need to trust your colleagues, just as you need to trust your manager. After all, you're all working toward the same goal.

GET ADVICE FROM SOMEONE WHO'S WHERE YOU WANT TO BE

Growing up playing basketball, I had a number of peers who seemed to be just a few steps or years ahead of me. I tended to follow their lead by playing for the same teams, going to the same camps, and pursuing the same college opportunities. One player whom I consistently followed—Chris Andrews—was two grades ahead of me, played point guard, and, like me, was from New Jersey. He and I attended the same high school for a time, played on the same team, and eventually became teammates at Yale. Chris was always a step ahead and blazed a trail that I could follow. I also tried to model some of my game off of his. He had quick hands, played excellent defense, was a vocal leader on and off the floor, and always gave 100%. All I had to do was try to replicate what Chris did, and I knew I'd be okay.

The impact his mentorship had on my growth and development as a player was immense, and when I landed my internship at Goldman Sachs, I immediately began looking for someone who could guide my professional career in the same ways Chris guided my playing career. It didn't take long to identify her. Edith Cooper was a very senior executive within the organization and, like me, African-American. She'd also worked in my division earlier in her career, so I knew she would be a good mentor for me.

One day, when we were both attending a company event, I summoned my courage and seized my chance. I approached her, introduced myself, and gave a quick elevator pitch detailing my background and how much I truly loved working there. She listened patiently and with interest, and I was excited when she requested that I follow up with her to book time on her calendar to continue the conversation. After all, she was a busy senior executive, and I was just an analyst. But I could tell that her interest was genuine, and I took her up on the offer.

She and I formed a bond that has endured over the course of my career. She quickly became a trusted advisor, an advocate, and a friend. I was able to feel comfortable with her being my mentor because she was very approachable and welcoming. Not everyone has the patience or desire to be a mentor, and it can be very intimidating for a younger employee to get to know a well-established figure within an organization, but I never got that with her. I thought that if she could accomplish all that she had done and was willing to listen to my story, there would be no better person to learn from—both during my career at Goldman and throughout the rest of my professional career.

The things she taught me have had an immeasurable impact on my career, and they still influence the work I do each day. If I were to list them, they could fill their own book, but these are a few lessons I return to most often:

BE PRESENT

As a senior executive, she had a million things on her plate each day. But whenever we met, she always took the time to listen to what I was saying. She never seemed distracted or impatient. Now that I'm running Jopwell, I always try to give my colleagues my undivided attention. Not only does this show that I respect what they have to say, but it also makes me a better listener—and a better leader.

BE HUMBLE

Despite being incredibly successful, she never seemed "above" or disinterested in the real-world challenges faced by her junior colleagues. She taught me the value of empathy, and it made communicating with her easy and comfortable.

BE HONEST

She never failed to tell me what I *needed* to hear, not what I *wanted* to hear. She didn't spare my feelings, and as a result, I always trusted her opinion and acted on it.

I can't imagine where I'd be without the mentors I've had. They've helped me advance my career by leaps and bounds, and the right mentor can do the same for you, too.

FIND YOUR MENTOR

To find the right mentor, start by examining which members of your organization's senior leadership are most likely able to help you develop and who can advocate for you when you want to take on special projects or are up for promotion.

Before you begin your search, identify what you'd like to gain from the relationship. If, for example, you work in IT but would eventually like to transition to a revenue-generating team, a VP of sales might be a great choice. If you want to grow within your current role, look for executives at the top of your function. Identify where you want to be in five or ten years' time and start taking steps toward building a relationship with someone who is already there.

In some large traditional organizations, a junior professional casually approaching a senior colleague is frowned upon. In others, it's completely acceptable. It's up to you to know your organization's culture and act appropriately.

Having clear objectives will also influence the elevator pitch you give when you approach your potential mentor. Prep yourself by crafting a thirty-second pitch that outlines who you are, where you want to go, and why this person is uniquely suited to mentor you. Tell them that you're aware of their busy schedule and that you aren't asking for a major time commitment. If you do this effectively, it's highly likely that they'll be more than happy to take you under their wing, even if they're incredibly busy. In my experience, people are generally willing to go out of their way to help those who ask.

Make a Performance Plan

Now that you understand what's required of you, have created a clear plan for building key relationships, and have taken steps toward securing a mentor, it's time to establish an outline for measurable professional growth.

Let's return to the basketball analogy for a moment. Every college team starts the season with the same long-term goal: winning the NCAA championship. But that game is five months away from the first

EMMITT SMITH'S WAY OF WINNING

Emmitt Smith isn't just a legendary running back. The former Dallas Cowboy is the NFL's all-time leading rusher, played in three Super Bowls, and has more awards to his name than most players can dream of. That's due, in large part, to his views on perseverance and success. His exceptional talent didn't hurt, of course, but plenty of players blessed with wonderful physical gifts never made it half as far. Smith's point of view is what differentiates him, which he explained best when he said, "Winning is something that builds physically and mentally every day that you train and every night that you dream."

Success doesn't happen overnight—or all at once. It's the cumulative result of *continuous* effort and focus. Remember that when you're feeling discouraged!

tip-off of the season, and a lot can happen in between. Key players get injured. Opponents who were expected to provide easy wins turn out to be a lot more threatening. Coaching staff leave.

With so many variables in play, the team that wins it all will be the one that not only has the right mix of talent and coaching, but also plans effectively for the season ahead. That includes breaking down long-term objectives into manageable and winnable short-term goals, like sticking to strict regimens—three or four weight-lifting sessions per week, no going out within forty-eight hours of a game, mandatory video review sessions—or implementing team-wide bonding sessions, like dinners after practice, to ensure a sense of family.

Once the short-term goals are determined, they can be further broken down into tasks on a checklist. This gives the team a step-by-step formula for success, as well as a method for measuring their progress and identifying opportunities for improvement.

This approach is also perfect for mapping out your career. Here's how.

Identify something you want to achieve this year. It could be earning a promotion, getting a raise, or even getting a new job at your current company. This should be an objective that, once achieved, benefits both you and your employer in a measurable way.

Determine the steps that must happen to make this objective a reality. These are now your short-term goals. If, say, you want to get promoted this year, ask yourself what must happen for that to take place. You might need to exceed your quarterly revenue targets, bring in new accounts, or demonstrate leadership qualities. Be realistic and avoid magical thinking here.

Create a checklist of tasks you need to perform to accomplish your short-term goals; for example, learning a new skill via a training course or creating a streamlined method for invoicing. No matter what you choose, make sure that crossing each one off your list brings you closer to achieving a short-term goal. Each item should represent real—not hypothetical or speculative—progress.

Keep yourself on track by setting ambitious but attainable deadlines. Break your year down into quarters, months, and weeks. When you miss a deadline, don't beat yourself up about it, but do understand why you missed it and how you can avoid letting that happen again.

It's important to make each goal as simple and straightforward as possible. You should be able to define each of the items just detailed in a single short sentence. If you can't, then the goal is too complex and you need to break it down into smaller steps. Additionally, your long-term objective should be achievable in no more than five short-term goals. If you can't achieve a long-term objective within those constraints, then it's not likely to happen. Reevaluate and establish a more attainable endgame.

To make this process easier, here's a template you can use. Minimal distractions and greater focus are critical for setting smart goals and holding yourself accountable.

- What is my long-term goal?
- How does this help me grow as a professional?
- How does this add value to my employer?
- What short-term goals do I need to accomplish to make this happen?
- Short-term goal #1 is: ______________________________ ____.
- How does this contribute to achieving my long-term goal?
- What am I going to do to make this happen?
- My due date(s) will be ____________.
- Short-term goal #2 is: ______________________________ ____.
- How does this contribute to achieving my long-term goal?
- What am I going to do to make this happen?
- My due date(s) will be ____________.
- Short-term goal #3: ________________________________ ____.
- How does this contribute to achieving my long-term goal?
- What am I going to do to make this happen?
- My due date(s) will be ____________.

Once you've filled this out and have a plan in place, set aside time each week to measure your progress. Be honest with yourself about your progress. It's inevitable that you'll make a mistake or miss a deadline somewhere along the way. But if you don't hold yourself accountable and, ideally, hold yourself accountable to others, you won't see results.

Last but not least, share this plan with your manager and mentor or even a trusted peer or two. Get their feedback on whether the plan is realistic and if there are ways to achieve your goals more efficiently.

Next, let's talk about how—and how not—to get recognized for all the work you do.

4

EARNING RECOGNITION FOR YOUR WORK

How to Turn the Work You Do into an Engine that Drives Your Career Forward

By setting short- and long-term goals and creating value within and outside of your job description, you've put yourself on the path to advancement. But somewhere between value creation and the next rung of the ladder lies a key variable: recognition. Contrary to what you may think, recognition isn't outside your control. It's not something others bestow upon you or that you should feel lucky to receive. Rather, it's something you earn, which means that as with goal setting, you can approach it strategically. You can *plan* for recognition.

First, what is recognition *not*? In an era of things going viral, of twenty-four-hour news cycles, and an endless supply of emerging pop-cultural touchstones, it may be hard to differentiate recognition from attention. But once you break it down, the differences are clear.

Attention is transient and fleeting. It doesn't require any action on the part of the person who bestows it; even as you read this, your attention is occasionally being diverted by the people around you.

Attention shines a brief light on you, but that's all it is: light. It can be earned or unearned; driven by positive, negative, or even neutral actions. Remember the spotlight effect—the sensation of extra attention derived from being different? Attention, especially the unearned variety, can be a distraction, diverting your focus away from what's really important and toward what others find noteworthy. It's based on someone else's definition of what's noteworthy, not your own, and it can create false expectations of future behavior.

Worse still, attention can be devalued or rescinded at any time. If you're a Millennial, you've probably encountered the stereotype that all members of our generation require attention, even if it's undeserved. After all, everyone gets a trophy just for participating, right? This dilutes the value of the attention you receive and undercuts whatever positive action you took to receive that attention.

Attention, then, is best left to YouTubers and those "doing it for the 'Gram."

But unlike attention, recognition is prompted by the creation of value. It requires proactive action on the part of the person who gives it, which means that it's far more likely to be earned than to be given at random. It arises from acts that add real, tangible value, rather than behaviors that others find interesting or noteworthy. After all, you're bound to receive attention for the errors you make, but you certainly won't be recognized for them.

Also, unlike most forms of attention, recognition drives subsequent action. That action may be an email noting your accomplishments, a mention at the next board meeting, or a promotion—regardless, it represents forward progress and often leaves some kind of evidence behind. It also means you can often use moments of recognition as a yardstick against which to measure your success.

So, as you work to create value, be mindful about whether the work you do is met with attention or recognition. Being able to spot the difference and plan accordingly could very well make or break your career.

How to Earn Recognition for Your Work

Based on the preceding discussion, you might be thinking: *Well, I know I'm doing good work and creating value, so why isn't the recognition rolling in from my peers and superiors?*

Unfortunately, the ratio of good work to recognition received is not one to one. In fact, according to a recent survey conducted by OGO (O Great One!), a firm that specializes in recognition coaching, 80% of employed Americans don't feel they're adequately recognized by their superiors.[47]

This is problematic for several reasons, the most important being the way it reduces productivity and creativity and contributes to mediocrity, thereby prompting even less recognition. Let's look at another statistic from that OGO survey: 40% of Americans say they would put in more effort if their work was recognized more often. That's a very large chunk of the American workforce not living up to its potential. And when a few coast—when they settle for good enough—they earn even less recognition, or worse, invite negative attention. They look bad, their managers look bad, and the business looks bad. It's not too difficult to imagine the large-scale consequences.

If you're a part of that 40%, I can understand why you might feel that putting in the extra work just isn't worth it. After all, you're not staying late to finish those projects just for your health. The good news, however, is that there's a solution to a lack of recognition. It just requires more strategic action on your part. The most difficult part will be taking the responsibility for recognition away from others and putting it on yourself. But once you accept that you have agency in the competition for recognition, the rest just seems like common sense.

Here's how to get started.

Understand What Recognition Looks Like

Part of the challenge of earning recognition is recognizing it when you get it. It comes in all shapes and sizes, which means you have to know what you're looking for. Once you've identified how your organization delivers it, you'll also need to decide whether you can work within those parameters.

For example, you may work at a company that delivers recognition in private meetings or one-on-ones, rather than in all-hands meetings. Your company may promote quickly when it comes to titles, but increased compensation may be slow to follow. Recognition may come in the form of more responsibility, a bigger team, or a focus on a niche service area.

Before you begin working to earn recognition, know what you're setting yourself up for and whether it aligns with your professional goals. You don't get to choose how you receive recognition, so be sure you understand how your organization recognizes contributions, and set your expectations accordingly. Or perhaps you need to find an organization that demonstrates recognition in a different way. The point is, the sooner you understand what you're in for, the better you can prepare.

IDENTIFY YOUR TARGET

It sounds a little obvious, but before you can earn recognition and the accompanying benefits, you have to know from whom you want to get it and the kinds of actions that will prompt it. This goes back to the "what, why, how, where" approach to your work we discussed in chapter 3, only now we're adding a "who" to the mix—as in who can help you achieve your short- and long-term goals?

Short term: Turn to your manager and peers. These are the people who can help you get promoted in the next year. If you're already focusing on adding value, then you're probably looking for "where" you can exceed expectations in your day-to-day performance. Well, look no further. Identify what's most important to your manager and/ or peers—their pain points, obstacles, and daily annoyances—and take proactive measures to solve those.

For example, if your manager has expressed concern with knowledge transfer between departments, consider establishing a cross-functional team that can open communication and share intelligence. If your peers are struggling to understand the tech behind a new product, work with your manager to get a lunchtime training session going. Remember, recognition doesn't have to entail a major effort. Often, it's the result of a series of small but valuable actions that add up over time.

Long term: Turn to your personal and professional networks. These are the people who can help you build your own brand. Rather than focus on solving problems, however, try to add extra value by deepening and enriching the network itself. You can do this by connecting like-minded members—for discussion, job referrals, interviews, and other opportunities. By spreading the social capital, you become a valued hub in the network, the go-to person when someone needs something—and that kind of recognition will initiate all the right introductions.

FIND A SPECIALTY

One way to add value is to solve problems no one else can. Is there a subject matter, process, or piece of technology stumping your manager or team members? Put in the extra hours not only to understand, but also to master it and offer your services to others. It's a quick way to stand out from the crowd, for both your expertise and your proactivity. This alone may not net you a promotion, but when combined with the other actions listed here, it certainly paints a very positive picture.

Communicate, Communicate, Communicate

You've identified how your organization delivers recognition, who the key "recognizers" are, and how you can best meet their needs. Now it's time to put your plan into action, and that means speaking up—and often. This may be the toughest part in this entire process. After all, you need to walk a fine line between self-advocacy and bragging, between acknowledging your work and hogging the credit.

The key here is honesty and open communication in all matters relating to recognition. Generally speaking, the more transparent you can be in all your communication, the better your chances of meaningful recognition without social fallout. Here's where and when you should overcommunicate.

WHEN YOU'RE SETTING EXPECTATIONS WITH YOUR MANAGER

Your manager is your direct channel to promotion, but to earn recognition from him or her, you need to be clear on a couple of points.

First, hearken back to the "what, why, how, where" methodology in chapter 3, specifically, the "where." Simply fulfilling your job description is probably not enough to get you recognition and promotion. Instead, ask where you can add extra value and be clear about deadlines and resources.

Second, be clear about what motivates you to succeed. You owe this to yourself as much as to your manager. If promotion is high on that list, find a way to discuss your career path. Ask direct questions. What can you do for the company? What can you do to get where you want to be professionally? You'll be equipping your manager with the tools they need to help you along on your journey, and that in and of itself will be appreciated.

WHEN ADVOCATING FOR YOURSELF

It's difficult to make progress in your career if you never raise your hand. By this I mean volunteering for new challenges, demonstrating expertise, and taking responsibility for a job well done—or an error made. By establishing a plan for recognition, you've already demonstrated self-advocacy. Now you have to execute fully by taking on those extra projects, generating valuable ideas, and owning your work. It's no small task, but you'll make it easier on yourself if you're transparent at every step.

When taking on new projects, make sure you're clear on the context, deadlines, stakeholders, and any other important points.

When you have an idea, answer, or solution, don't be afraid to voice it, but be choosy. Before you present it, know what it is about your proposal that makes it better than the rest. Be ready to show your work; unless your team leader specifically asks for any and all ideas, present only your best.

If you receive praise for a project, don't demur or shift credit to other people. Accept the recognition graciously and be clear that you welcome any other feedback, positive or negative. If you messed up, the same rules apply. Trust me—transparency will win the day here.

WHEN SHARING CREDIT

Of course, if your work is the product of a group effort, be sure to share the praise with your team members, even if you are the team leader. Self-advocacy is important, but be wary of crossing over into glory hogging. That will only backfire on you, as your boss begins to lose trust in you, and your peers shy away from working with you on important projects. When preparing to accept praise, know ahead of time who contributed what, and why that contribution was important to the overall success of the project.

If, however, you are leading a team that fails in some way, that's not the time to assign blame. As the leader, you're responsible for the final product. Acknowledge the failure, find a solution, and be clear about how you're going to prevent it from happening next time.

DON'T WAIT

A critical mistake that many young professionals make, especially those new to an organization, is waiting until their annual review to highlight their accomplishments. That's too little, too late. To stay visible, you need to highlight your achievements early and often. Your boss probably won't do it for you. According to the OGO survey, U.S. employees reported an average of fifty days since they had been last recognized at work.[48]

Find a way to work your successes into your weekly one-on-ones with your manager. If you have a meeting agenda, note it there as a win. Be prepared to show the work that went into that win and share credit if it was a group effort.

Find ways to leverage the work you did as part of that win in other projects. The more you can use the expertise you gain, the more value you'll add, and the more visible your success will remain.

TRACK EVERYTHING

Your weekly meeting agenda isn't the only place to note your accomplishments. Be sure to keep detailed records of the work you did on each project. That includes:

- Any special training, certification programs, or other education in which you participated, especially if it took place outside regular working hours
- Information or expertise you sought from individuals outside your department
- Extra hours worked
- Unique ways in which you made use of company resources
- Collaborations you initiated
- Money spent versus money saved
- Long- and short-term value added to the organization
- Potential future utilizations of the products, processes, skills, or resources you developed

Keep these in a document, and update them weekly. Refer to them as necessary, but at the very least, bring them up during annual or quarterly reviews.

VALIDATE YOURSELF FIRST

This is a big one, and while it may seem counterintuitive at first, it really is the key to earning meaningful recognition that pays long-term dividends.

Say you just closed a major deal at the end of the quarter, enabling your manager to boast to her manager that your team made its quota in the nick of time. That's a great win. Now, imagine that your manager does not mention that it was your sale that put the team over the edge. That's not so great. It might be tempting to find a way to tell your boss's boss about your success or to vent to your teammates about your manager's blind spot when it comes to giving due credit. After all, we just talked about the need to self-advocate when it comes to recognition.

In this situation, however, do neither. There will be times when your work goes unpraised. Your manager is a human, and humans are imperfect creatures. Chances are she's not trying to slight you—her focus is just elsewhere.

That's not to say you don't address the issue.

First and foremost, you have to be able to find validation for your achievements within yourself. Tracking the work that went into each is a good way to start. It helps you quantify the effort and chart your growth as a professional.

Second, if you're not already working with a mentor, find one now. One function of a mentor is providing guidance on your growth and development, so they expect to be kept in the loop on your accomplishments. A mentor can help validate if your manager doesn't—and will make sure that others in your industry know what you've achieved.

Finally, if your manager doesn't acknowledge your work right away, try to find another way to bring it up. Maybe you can repurpose part of your project for another initiative. Maybe the certification you got in order to complete this project can be applied elsewhere. Properly managed, the value you've created will snowball through your department, and that will be noticed. And there's always your annual review.

What to Do If You're Truly Not Being Recognized

If you've completed all of these steps, continued to produce exceptional work, and are still not receiving the recognition you think you've earned, there may be other factors at play. Fortunately, you can address each, though it won't be easy. Here are four factors to look for.

YOUR WORK REALLY ISN'T ALL THAT EXCEPTIONAL

It's not an easy thing to admit, but if you've advocated for yourself, tracked your achievements, maintained open and honest communication, and are getting nothing in return, it's time to take a look at your output. Really look. Ask yourself, your manager, and, ideally, your mentor, "Does my work actually merit recognition?"

Be prepared for a tough answer. It may be that you need to spend more time educating yourself on your organization's product or service. Maybe you've been focusing on areas that don't align with upper management's priorities. It's okay; this is how you improve. But you do have to improve. Trying won't get you the gold star it might have in elementary school. The good thing is, by surfacing your concerns with your manager, you're more likely to be recognized when you do start producing excellent work.

YOUR MANAGER DOESN'T UNDERSTAND THE VALUE OF WHAT YOU'RE DOING

Whenever I see this happen, it's generally because the work you're doing isn't obviously tied to a strategic business objective. They can't see how your achievements have moved the needle, and if they can't see it, they certainly can't articulate it to someone higher up the ladder.

TO KEEP YOUR ENERGY UP, RECOGNIZE YOUR OWN CONTRIBUTIONS

Learning to self-validate can be tough. Most of us are raised not to boast about our accomplishments or draw attention to ourselves—and rightfully so, I think. But, when it comes to professional success, it's important to be able to validate yourself for a variety of reasons. Here are some ways you can recognize your own success, even if your manager or colleagues aren't showing you the love you feel you deserve:

Keep a running list of your accomplishments and quantify the impact they've had on the company. If, for example, you saved the company money or time by fixing a broken process, try to calculate the dollar amount you saved. That's a great way to prove to yourself that you've done great work with meaningful impact—and it'll come in handy for your next review.

Maintain a thorough to-do list and check things off as you go. Seeing your progress on paper is motivating and keeps you energized. Capture even simple tasks, such as sending a follow-up email or reviewing a proposal. Review your list at the end of each day to remind yourself of all the great work you've done.

Set realistic goals. You should always aim high, but setting unattainable goals is a great way to burn out. You might want to be the company's top salesperson within your first six months, but it'll take time to learn the company, its products or services, and your customers' wants and needs. Instead of trying to lead the pack right away, set a realistic goal that sets you up to be the leading salesperson by the end of your first year.

This situation demands another form of self-advocacy—a thoughtful and explicit business case for your work. Never assume that your manager can see inside your head. Make sure they understand the value of your work by mapping each project or initiative to a specific and meaningful business outcome. Make it clear in advance that you'd like the chance to review your work to date and its impact on the business. Present your analysis at your one-on-one meeting and be sure to have as much data as possible to back up your claims.

While you'll need to perform extra work, the initiative you show in putting together this analysis should earn you some recognition in addition to what you'll receive based on your previous projects. Going forward, consider putting together a miniature version of this presentation before every new project you undertake. That way your manager will have a clear idea of your work, can help you measure progress against goals, and can report on your achievements in a timely manner.

YOUR COMPANY DOESN'T RECOGNIZE PEOPLE EFFECTIVELY

Unfortunately, not all companies and managers are good at recognizing achievement in meaningful ways. Maybe no one's ever thought through a system for formal recognition. Or maybe there *is* one, but managers are too taxed with other priorities to execute.

If you suspect this might be the problem, do some research. Speak to your human resources rep or head of people. Read through your employee handbook. If there is a documented process in place, schedule some time with your manager and, ideally, a member of human resources to discuss implementation. Try not to focus on the problem of lack of recognition in the past and definitely don't make it about getting recognition for yourself. Instead, engage your manager in a discussion of team-wide motivation and the importance of demonstrating that the organization values your team's work.

There are plenty of statistics that show a correlation between motivated, engaged employees and higher retention. For example, in one 2016 survey of human resources professionals by the Society for Human Resource Management and Globoforce, 88% of those surveyed said that an investment of at least 1% of payroll in recognition and reward programs correlated with a strong return on investment and better retention rates.[49] Chances are your human resources rep has their own statistics on hand. Don't be afraid to lean on them to help make your case.

FAVORITISM OR DISCRIMINATION (OR BOTH) ARE AT WORK

Last, but certainly not least, there is always the possibility that some form of favoritism or discrimination is at play in your department, or even across the organization. If you consistently witness others receiving recognition for contributions equal to or less than yours, while you never receive the same, it's time to have a frank conversation with your manager.

Go in prepared, with as many instances as possible documented. If you don't feel comfortable handling the meeting by yourself, bring a human resources rep with you. Point to the instances you've documented and ask your manager why it continues to happen. Be candid but not accusatory. There could be an explanation, but if you immediately put your manager on the defensive, you probably won't get a straightforward answer. If, on the other hand, your manager can't offer a satisfactory explanation, then the unfortunate reality is that it may be time for you to start looking for a new job. Or, if your human resources department is strong, your manager will have to answer for the points you've raised and address your concerns.

Whatever you do, don't let this experience haunt you in your next gig. Use it as a learning experience; be prepared; be circumspect. But more than anything else, be ready to advocate for yourself and your team members. Your organization will be better off for it, and so will you.

How to Handle Recognition Once You Have It

Congratulations! You've delivered a successful project or projects, and your manager has rewarded you with recognition. Enjoy what you've earned, but resist the urge to kick back and wait for a parade in your honor. Once you've gotten recognition, your work has only begun. Here's how to nurture it until it grows into a promotion.

HAVE PATIENCE

It's a rare workplace indeed that follows a first job well done with instant promotion. Don't expect to be vaulted up the ladder after a single successful project, or even a quarter's worth. If recognition is the short game, promotion is the long. Continued overachievement, open communication, and self-advocacy must be part of your playbook even after the first glow of validation.

That said, don't be afraid to set timelines with your manager. Work with them to document a plan for advancement that satisfies both your needs, and be sure to set mutually agreed-upon milestones and check-ins along the way.

MAINTAIN REASONABLE EXPECTATIONS

As I mentioned earlier, organizations recognize achievement in different ways. Depending on the size of the company, senior titles may come along more quickly than increased compensation. Advancement may mean a larger group of people for you to manage. Understand how and when your organization recognizes achievement and manage your expectations accordingly. This will help you avoid disappointment and burnout.

SHARE THE CREDIT

Here's another one I've already discussed, but it remains as important on day 671 as it does on Day One. The more recognition you earn and the higher you advance, the more difficult it may be to remember to give credit where it's due. But remember, those you take credit from now may be the ones tasked with doling out rewards later. Teams work better when each member feels valued. So stay transparent about who did what and when. This act alone will help you shine.

Before we close this discussion, let's address one big, glowing caveat: the importance of good work for good work's sake. Yes, recognition is important for getting promoted and growing your career and personal brand. But it shouldn't be the driving force behind your desire to do great work. It's an outcome, not a reason. Take pride in your own accomplishments, even if they go unnoticed, and don't lose heart if you're not getting the recognition you feel you deserve. Take action, but remember that you're the manager of your own self-worth.

5

BUILDING A POWERFUL PERSONAL BRAND

Why You Need a Personal Brand at Work, and How to Build One

Hard as it may be to believe, one of the world's biggest and most ubiquitous personal brands actively resisted the notion that she was, in fact, a brand—for many, many years—until a chance encounter with a woman in a grocery store changed her mind. The fan, a mother, told her that it was her influence that had led the fan to stop hitting her child as a form of punishment. The personal brand is, of course, Oprah. The billionaire media mogul told attendees at a 2015 QuickBooks Connect conference that once she had come to understand what branding was, she embraced it.[50] For her, building a personal brand meant identifying key principles or values and sticking to them. It also meant being clear on one's own intentions. Oprah became famous for requiring transparency from the guests on her talk show, and from herself. She wasn't afraid to tell them when she had brought them on her show to satisfy a personal mission—for example, to shed light on domestic abuse by highlighting a victim's story on-air with the victim's family present.

You don't need to build a vast media and lifestyle empire to have a personal brand. Anyone can develop one. What's important is that you do, and once you do, that you act consistent with that brand. In this chapter, we'll examine just why personal branding is important to all professionals, especially POC. We'll explore ways you can define your brand and nurture it to help you grow in your career. Finally, we'll discuss the importance of brand evolution.

But first, what exactly is a personal brand?

Your Personal Brand

In 1997, business management author and speaker Tom Peters wrote in *Fast Company*: "We are CEOs of our own companies: Me Inc. To be in business today, our most important job is to be head marketer for the brand called You."[51]

Thought to be the coiner of the term "personal branding," Peters advocated for building a personal and professional reputation in much the same way the brand managers at companies like Nike or Starbucks went about building theirs. Trustworthiness, consistency, key differentiators—these were just as important in the individual as they were in giant brands. If you wanted to succeed in business, you'd start by marketing yourself.

Think of your personal brand as an amalgam of your public behavior, which you leverage as a representation of your values. It's your reputation, sure, but it's also all the things you do that define and differentiate you from others. It's unique to you, and, to an extent, you nurture it by the actions you take and don't take.

In some ways, Peters's words foreshadowed the rise of the ultimate self-branding tool: social media. Thanks to Facebook, Twitter, Instagram, Snapchat, and LinkedIn, we may be more cognizant than ever before of how we appear to the rest of the world. But if being aware of image is sharing a bunch of photos from a networking event, then building and maintaining a brand is curating a few choice photos of yourself with fellow movers-and-shakers, captioned with a key insight. In other words, there's a right way and a wrong way to go about branding yourself.

Why Everyone Needs a Personal Brand

The benefits of self-branding vary from person to person. You build your brand, which means you can tailor it toward a specific goal or objective. It serves your unique needs. But there are a few ways in which simply having a brand can help you as you grow your career. Keep in mind, these benefits are associated with positive personal brands. If your brand goes off track, then you won't necessarily achieve the desired outcomes.

INFLUENCE

We create 2.5 quintillion bytes of data every day. Billions of pieces of content. Included in that are professional bios, résumés, About Us pages, personal websites, emails, social media posts, news articles, webinars, blog posts, and instant messages. The list goes on. The point is, it's becoming harder and harder for the average professional to be heard above the noise, at least online.

But a brand is different. A brand can develop an image and voice that, over time and with consistent messaging, becomes wholly its own. By developing a personal brand, you differentiate yourself from the billions of others clamoring for a piece of the world's attention. And a brand that differentiates itself is a brand that wields influence.

Consider the example of Oprah. She was able to build her empire by embodying a specific set of values that she upheld over and over again. She delivered value in multiple layers. And by being transparent about her intentions, she carved out a space in broadcast television. There's only one Oprah—her brand is utterly unique, it drives conversation, it persuades others to explore her point of view, and, ultimately, it creates profit. It's unlikely many of us will develop a personal brand as powerful as Oprah's, but nevertheless she is a great example of how far a strong personal brand can take you in work—and in life.

ADAPTABILITY

It seems as if every day another article is published on some radical shift in the way we work. From artificial intelligence and automation to the rise of the gig economy, what it means to be an employee is in constant flux, which means that we have to keep reinventing ourselves over and over again.

Reinvention is easier when you're actively engaged in brand building. Developing a personal brand starts with identifying a persona, an inventory of your qualities, some careful planning, and then specific and ongoing action. When the market shifts, when priorities change, the self-brander simply changes the plan. By being tapped into your values, by knowing your strengths and weaknesses, you can more easily pivot to find what works best in the context of the market.

NARRATIVE

People connect with stories. A personal brand takes what's on your résumé or LinkedIn page and crafts a narrative, which provides detail that a list of previous jobs and degrees simply can't capture—things like intent, drive, priorities, leadership capacity, and proactivity.

A brand narrative is something you can take into any interview or networking event; it captures attention instantly and quickly and efficiently provides dimension and context. Later in this chapter, we'll walk through creating that narrative.

The Importance of Personal Brands for POC

More than a decade after Peters wrote about branding oneself, personal branding experts David McNally and Karl Speak defined personal brand as "a perception or emotion, maintained by somebody other than you, that describes the total experience of having a relationship with you."[52]

That clause in the middle—"maintained by somebody other than you"—is the most critical part of the definition. While you build and shape your personal brand, ultimately it exists in the minds of others. Which, for POC, makes branding especially critical.

Why? Remember the spotlight effect. As a person of color, you'll receive extra attention and scrutiny just for being different. Everything you do in your professional—and sometimes your personal—life will have consequences for the way you are perceived. Being proactive about your personal brand will allow you to better direct that attention, but you'll need to be careful in how you craft your image.

Is that unfair? Well, sure, but it's also an opportunity. Focus on your brand early in your career, stay consistent, and you can take advantage of that extra attention to excel. Conversely, if you stray from your narrative or if you create a weak or negative brand experience, you're apt to draw the wrong kind of attention. And that can have serious consequences.

Here's how to start brand-building the right way.

Defining Your Personal Brand

In that seminal article on personal branding, Tom Peters had the following advice for professionals:

> *To start thinking like your own favorite brand manager, ask yourself the same question the brand managers at Nike, Coke, Pepsi, or the Body Shop ask themselves: What is it that my product or service does that makes it different? Give yourself the traditional 15-words-or-less contest challenge. Take the time to write down your answer. And then take the time to read it. Several times.*
>
> *If your answer wouldn't light up the eyes of a prospective client or command a vote of confidence from a satisfied past client, or—worst of all—if it doesn't grab you, then you've got a big problem.*[53]

Peters is going for a dramatic effect here, but he's not wrong about the process. A brand story should be rich and full of detail, but you must also be able to summarize it in as few words as possible. Your brand is an elevator pitch for the value you bring to a potential employer or organization. The best way to hone your personal brand is by identifying your strengths, connecting them to four or five traits, crafting a persona around them, and then observing how closely that mirrors the personal brands of the senior-most POC in your organization.

IDENTIFY YOUR STRENGTHS

If you want to build a brand, you need to think like a marketer or brand manager, which means you'll need to do some research on yourself. It's not enough to have a vague idea of stuff you're good at.

Your strengths form the foundation of your brand and should inform and help build the traits around which you craft that brand.

There's another reason you need to have a clear idea of what you're best at before you begin to brand yourself: efficiency. Don't waste time trying to pursue the wrong brand. By "wrong" I mean a brand that's rooted in something you're not. There's no point in billing yourself as, say, an aggressive dealmaker if it's just not in your nature to be aggressive. There will always be areas to work on, traits you can develop and improve, but if you're starting at zero, that may indicate that this is a trait that's not worth pursuing.

If you're not sure where to start when it comes to self-assessment, try a personality test—a real one, not a quiz about what kind of nineties kid you are. Two options I like are the Myers-Briggs Type Indicator (MBTI) and the Riso-Hudson Enneagram Type Indicator (RHETI).

While the personality tests differ, each can help you identify a core personality type by assessing your likely behavior in different situations. Your identified personality type encompasses both strengths and weaknesses in areas such as independent thinking, approval seeking, proactivity, creativity, and organization skills.

Now, a big caveat: Personality tests, while useful for creating a snapshot, are not comprehensive. They can inform your brand, but you shouldn't fall into the trap of reverse-engineering everything you do to fit your assigned type. Resist the urge to say, "Well, I'm a visionary type, so I should approach problems only with ultra-creative, big-idea solutions." You're more complex than that (and that's a good thing). Factor your test results into a brand persona that *you* name, not the other way around.

Let's say your self-assessment surfaces strengths in the following areas:

- Knowledgeable
- Quick-thinking
- Original
- Charismatic
- Energetic
- Strong brainstorming skills

These happen to be the strengths associated with the ENTP type in the Myers-Briggs Type Indicator assessment.[54] However you choose to assess yourself, try to reduce the results to a concise list; you'll be able to expand on them later. For now, we'll take these strengths and compare them to a new list: your traits.

DEFINE YOUR BRAND TRAITS

Your brand traits are the tent poles around which you'll craft a fully fleshed-out personal brand. Once set, you should be able to list these in any job interview, introductory email, or personal bio. Like your strengths assessment, this list should comprise single words and short phrases.

For example, when defining my own personal brand, I use the following terms:

- Honest
- Direct
- Leader
- Respectful
- Dependable
- Loyal

I'd like to think of my brand in these terms, as I think these words lead people to trust me and want to be on my team—or support me in my career. I'm a very transparent person, and I say what I mean and mean what I say, so people always know where they stand with me. I think it's a sign of respect to treat everyone as equals. I also place a lot of value on people sticking to their word and, if they give an ETA on an assignment, sticking to it. Being dependable is so important in building trust and providing the necessary confidence for people to want to follow you.

With that in mind, ask yourself: How do you want others to see you? As an innovative thought leader? A hard-core, sales-focused rainmaker? An organized, hyperefficient problem solver? Make a list of five to seven traits, each no more than two or three words. Some traits may overlap with the strengths you identified during your self-assessment. That's great, but it doesn't mean there isn't work to do in learning how to use those strengths to create a brand.

Let's continue with the example just presented. Say your goal is to be seen by others as the following:

- Driven
- Strategic thinker
- Confident
- Efficient
- Problem solver
- Inspiring

These happen to be the traits associated with the ENTJ type on the Myers-Briggs assessment. There's nothing wrong with looking to their inherent traits for inspiration. So, how do those traits compare to the strengths we listed in the prior step? Identify the following.

- Areas of overlap: Where are your strengths and goals naturally in sync?
- Areas of support: How can your strengths support and help you achieve the goals that don't overlap?
- Areas of divergence: Where are the gaps between your strengths and your goals?

Using our example, the only area of overlap is charismatic/inspiring. You're already someone who can capture a room and sway others to your point of view. Depending on the content of your message, it's very easy to translate that quality into inspiration. Well done.

There are more areas of support than areas of overlap. Being knowledgeable—in other words, being a self-motivated, lifelong learner—as well as a quick and original thinker can support strategy, problem solving, even efficiency. High energy supports drive. The point is, there are numerous ways in which your strengths can support your efforts to build your brand traits.

Now let's talk areas of divergence. It's timc for some radical honesty with yourself. Chances are, those traits that are most supported by your existing strengths are the ones that people already recognize in you. The ones least supported are most likely those least recognized. So which traits are the furthest from your current brand? Which will require development of nonexistent or nascent skills? In our example, drive is one trait that, while supported by energy, may necessitate extra effort to establish; you may already possess it, but others may not see it. The same goes for confidence. When it comes to building your brand, you'll need to focus the most on these traits.

CREATE A PROFILE

But before you build your brand, you need to create a profile, or a persona, as traditional marketers would call it. Strengths and traits are essential, but they don't exactly grab the imagination. To better help you and those around you visualize your goals, take some time to flesh out the details. Think of your brand in terms of a book or movie character. How would you describe it in a trailer or on the back cover of a bestseller? There are many ways to package your brand. Using my example, you might describe yours as follows.

The Decision-Maker: A powerful and dynamic thinker, she always commands the room, finds long-term solutions to big problems, and can persuade others to see things her way. She approaches her goals the same way, playing the long game, planning for and overcoming all obstacles in her way.

Others may craft personas that are more tactical or job-based; for example.

The Rainmaker: Sales focused and always professional, he's willing to go the distance for his deal, literally and figuratively. He always makes his numbers but offers extra value in the sales insights and best practices he brings to his team.

Still others may craft personas that are tactical and skills-based.

The Fixer: Meticulously organized and efficient, she's adept at keeping many balls in the air at once while still being effective at her job. She's often the first to try new digital tools that help her work more effectively, and she's always willing to help others get organized and find efficiencies.

The point is, you need to find the profile that works best for you. It should (1) be achievable with a little bit of stretching, (2) have a foundation in your current strengths with room for growth, and (3) be easy to communicate to others. Once you've established that, you're ready to start building your brand.

Building Your Personal Brand

Building a personal brand is not that much different from building or marketing a commercial brand. There are specific steps to take, each driven by a particular goal or objective. The difference is, while you can create a commercial brand from nothing, a personal brand must be deeply rooted in who you are. Otherwise, at best, you'll be seen as inauthentic, and at worst, you'll fail to meet your goals altogether.

Luckily, in defining your brand, you've already done a lot of the heavy lifting. Now it's time to lay out the steps you'll need to take to build out each of your traits. If it helps you to visualize your goals, consider creating a personal brand matrix by creating a chart with rows for each trait (My Trait) and columns indicating the strengths you're already applying to those traits (Strengths I've Mastered); strengths you have but need to nurture (Strengths I'm Nurturing); those you need to develop entirely (Strengths I Need to Develop); and personal or professional opportunities to apply, nurture, or develop those strengths (Opportunities to Apply or Develop).

Here's where your mentor can help—first, as a gut check that the brand you're trying to build is in sync with who you are as a person and a professional, and second, by helping identify opportunities to apply your strengths and build those traits in the workplace. Start with a results-oriented approach, by which I mean working with your mentor to describe the results you need to achieve in order to demonstrate ownership of each of your traits.

The low-hanging fruit here is, of course, the quantifiable stuff: sales quotas, revenue goals, or budget savings. But even if your role is not tied to dollars and cents, you can still set results-oriented goals that will help you strengthen your personal brand.

In the preceding example, you've identified strategic thinking and problem solving as two goals. You might want to look for organization-wide issues that require proactive thinking and participation from multiple departments. Next, work with your manager to put together an action plan that includes leadership of an interdepartmental committee charged with finding a solution. Be diligent and organized; document each meeting, the solutions offered, and follow-up items. Note your own participation, but be sure to give credit to others as well.

This is just one example. All the steps don't have to be that big. Work with your mentor to identify other ways you can more closely align yourself with the brand trait you've established. It may be a matter of changing small behaviors, such as:

- Arriving to work early or on time every day
- Creating efficiencies to streamline processes
- Meeting deadlines every time
- Highlighting colleagues' achievements
- Dressing more professionally

By linking concrete workplace objectives to each trait, you can create six-month, one-year, and even multiyear plans for personal brand building. Remember to document each milestone achieved and be sure to raise these examples to your manager at your reviews; the more managerial buy-in you can get now, the easier each subsequent step will be.

Leveraging Your Brand Online

There's one major misstep many young professionals make when building a brand: inconsistency. Your personal brand isn't just a costume you put on in the morning and take off when you get home. It's a way of being. Everything you say and do at work, around members of your network, and online influences how you and your brand are perceived.

Let me repeat: *Everything you do online influences how you and your brand are perceived.* Your social media and forum posts, your texts, your emails—it all counts. Which means you can use your digital presence to help build your brand—or to tear it down.

Think about how closely a marketing team manages a company's messaging. Marketers craft a brand's social media calendar weeks ahead of time, and when a situation arises that demands a quick post, there is often an approval flow that social copy must move through before it hits the internet. For some brands, this approach has resulted in a well-crafted image that helps drive customer engagement. Consider MoonPie, based in Chattanooga, Tennessee. The hundred-plus-year-old company has garnered a lot of social media attention for a Twitter account that is deeply rooted in millennial and Gen Z humor, makes intelligent use of well-known internet tropes, and never takes itself very seriously. In fact, MoonPie hired an agency to specifically handle social media, and in doing so, it has boosted sales and awareness for a brand that has otherwise changed little in the last century.[55]

Conversely, those that ignore their online branding, even for a day, court disaster. For example, the dating app Tinder made headlines when it was cited as a contributing factor in the rise of hookup culture. When the journalist who wrote the article tweeted a particularly damning statistic—that 30% of Tinder users are married—the app's social media account erupted, sending a barrage of angry tweets to the journalist and thereby drawing more attention to an already negative public relations situation.[56] Other Twitter users piled on Tinder; journalists picked up the tweetstorm and generally mocked the brand; and, as of this writing, Tinder has yet to completely shed its image as a hookup facilitation app.[57]

I bring up these examples not to praise one brand or excoriate another but to demonstrate how brands that pour money into marketing and social media are affected by their online branding. The same is true for your personal brand. It's not enough to put an opinion disclaimer in your Twitter bio. You need to be thoughtful about all your messaging and ensure that, at the very least, it's always aligned with your traits. Beyond that, social media can be extremely useful for building and leveraging your brand outside your place of work. As you get ready to post that next photo or comment on someone's story, ask yourself:

- Is this post consistent with the traits I have set for myself?
- Will this post move me closer to my brand goals or set me back?
- Am I engaging with others out of emotion, or do I really have something useful to contribute to the conversation?
- Am I engaging with the right individuals and organizations online?
- How can I be both visible and valuable within my online network? Can I help connect people or foster dynamic discussion?
- Am I demonstrating my expertise and skill set effectively?
- Do I need to scrub older posts that are not aligned with my branding strategy?
- How can I use social media to build a narrative, connecting my past accomplishments to my current engagements and future plans?

Let's be honest—you won't always use social media for brand building. Sometimes you'll just want to have fun, and that's perfectly fine. But even if you're not actively advancing your personal brand on your social platform of choice, your words will be perceived as part of it. It's simple: if your personal brand is important to you, avoid whatever might erase the hard work you've put into creating it.

Evolving Your Brand over Time

You've created personal branding goals and established a plan for fulfilling them, and you're managing your brand online and off. You've done well. But there's one last element to keep in mind: change.

We've already touched on the need to stay flexible in your branding plan—to allow for external variations that might impact your objectives. It's also critical to think about the changes your brand will and should undergo in the long term. Your personal brand today should not look the same five years from now. You're going to grow and evolve with age, and your brand should follow suit.

I'm not advocating an overhaul every few years; the bedrock traits of your brand should remain somewhat constant. But you may choose to add some new ones, deprioritize others, and apply them in different ways. And yes, every once in a while, if circumstances dictate it, you may need to do a little reinventing. But that doesn't mean you abandon the best of what got you to where you are.

We started this chapter discussing one of the world's most famous personal brands. Whether or not you personally admire Oprah, it's hard to deny that she's been wildly successful at finding new and interesting ways to apply the core traits of her brand across a decades-long career. There's no reason you can't do the same—and have a lot of success along the way.

6

BECOMING AND REMAINING YOUR AUTHENTIC SELF

How to Bring the Real You to Work Every Day

Over the past three chapters, we've built a blueprint for success. Setting goals, having a plan for creating value, understanding when and how to get recognized for your contributions, and building a powerful personal brand are all key steps that drive your career forward. But there's one last step you'll need to complete: learning to bring your authentic self to work every day.

No matter how well you perform or how much recognition you receive, you won't achieve your full potential if you can't be who you are—who you *really* are—at work, day in and day out.

POC know this all too well. Because we're often one of the few representatives of our communities in the workplace—and sometimes we're the only one—we may feel as if our authentic selves are unwanted or unwelcome. In talking to hundreds of business leaders at companies ranging from startups to major enterprise-level organizations, I've found that in most cases, the opposite is true. Most businesses want, welcome, and encourage diverse perspectives and experiences because they recognize the value they deliver. But despite these businesses' best efforts to invest in creating spaces where everyone feels comfortable being who they are, it can still be difficult for POC to feel at ease being their authentic selves.

The reasons are varied and complex, but at the most basic level, there are two primary factors. The first stems from decades of institutionalized racism. During much of the twentieth century, our authentic selves—our thoughts, feelings, opinions, and experiences—weren't welcomed at work. Employers often expected us to conform to our majority colleagues, and POC couldn't get ahead or, in some cases, even maintain employment unless they assimilated.

Our parents and grandparents experienced it, and many of today's young professionals likely saw and heard their fears and anxieties expressed around the dinner table. I'd even wager that a sizable portion of young professionals of color even had some version of the "tone it down at work" talk with their parents at some point. While this is no longer the case in most workplaces, it's unrealistic to expect us to instantly overcome a behavior learned through generations of institutionalized bias.

Another reason we often hesitate to share our whole selves with our colleagues is the fear that they won't understand or share our values, tastes, and perspectives. This kind of behavior isn't limited to POC. When we're around people who are different from us, most of us tend to be a little more reserved. As normal as that may be, it prevents us from engaging with our coworkers and building valuable relationships. Of course, there are those who harbor stigmas, to whom you'll never feel connected, but you still have to be able to be yourself around them.

There's a perfect example cited in a recent *Harvard Business Review* article entitled simply "Diversity and Authenticity":[58]

> *Consider a woman we'll call Karen, a well-educated professional working in higher education, who recalls a conversation at a birthday party her colleagues threw for her. A white coworker asked, "What did you do for your birthday?" Karen replied, "I went to a concert with my husband and some friends." The coworker asked the logical follow-up question: "Who did you see?" Karen had seen Kirk Franklin, an African-American gospel artist who's quite popular among her black friends. She assumed the colleague wouldn't be familiar with Franklin, so she mumbled, "You won't know him" and pivoted to a new topic. This may sound like an innocuous exchange, but years later Karen remembers it as significant: "If I am not comfortable with who I am, the music I like, the places I like to go, how can I expect my coworker to value me for who I am? What is so wrong with being excited about Kirk Franklin?"*

The answer, of course, is "nothing." There's nothing wrong with liking Kirk Franklin, and I doubt her colleague would think so, either. But Karen's anxieties about potentially having to explain who Kirk Franklin is and what his music is like prevented her from opening up and truly engaging with her coworker. That was a terrific opportunity to bond and grow closer with her peer, but she feared being judged or feeling even more alienated than usual. She also, in retrospect, hit the nail squarely on the head: her coworker won't ever value her for who she is if she doesn't open up.

If you're a person of color, this exchange likely feels very familiar to you. Opening up to your colleagues can be stressful, even for the most gregarious, extroverted professionals. But it's also critical, not just for your sanity but also for your career—and your employer.

MICHELLE OBAMA'S RADICAL AUTHENTICITY

There's no shortage of reasons to admire former first lady Michelle Obama. Her drive, passion, intellect, and compassion are all exemplary, but her authenticity is also truly inspiring. She's never someone she's not, no matter how high the stakes are or how formal the occasion. That goes a long way in explaining why so many, myself included, consider her a role model.

How to Be Your Best Self

Matthew 5:15 tells us: "No one lights a lamp and puts it under a basket, but rather on a lampstand, and it gives light for all who are in the house."

That analogy holds true for the world of work, too—no one who wants to be successful shows up to work and fails to give 100%. And yet, while we may put our all into our projects, many of us do hide our light when it comes to our work relationships; we withhold elements of ourselves from our colleagues. That means we're not truly giving everything we have to add value for our employers and to drive our careers forward.

I know firsthand that being who you are in a workplace where you're one of a few POC is anything but easy. Here are some actionable steps that make it easier for us—and everyone—to be our best and authentic selves, open up, and stop hiding our light at work.

WHAT IS YOUR "SELF" ANYWAY?

Before we go any further, let's try an exercise. Answer the following questions in a couple of sentences each.

How do you see yourself? This includes your personality traits, physical characteristics, and anything that makes up the way you view yourself.

Who is the person you want to become? This is the person you wish you were or are striving to become. Again, this may include personality traits, physical characteristics, values, and work ethic.

How do you value yourself? What do you consider valuable about yourself and why? Are there other ways you want to value yourself?

Hang on to these answers. We're going to come back to them shortly.

Before we can truly be ourselves, we need to be clear about what "self" means in this context. The answer is surprisingly complex.

There are a number of definitions of "selfhood" out there, but one of the most common among psychologists is the late Carl Rogers's "self-concept" model. Rogers's model breaks the self-concept down into three distinct components.

Your self-image: How you see yourself, both inside and out. For example, do you consider yourself attractive or unattractive? Are you a good person or a bad person? Moral or immoral?

Your self-worth: The amount of value you ascribe to yourself. Are you a valuable member of society? An important part of your family? A key contributor at work?

Your ideal self: The person you wish you were. Do you wish you were more physically fit? Better read? More assertive at work?

To be our best selves, Rogers believed, our self-image and ideal-self should be as closely aligned as possible. In other words, if the person you believe yourself to be and the person you want to be are closely aligned, you're much more likely to be happy and ascribe yourself greater self-worth.[59]

Now, let's look back at your answers to the questions. How similar are your answers to the first two questions? If they're quite similar, then you probably value yourself highly. If they're radically different, however, it's a safe bet that your self-worth is relatively low—and that's what you should focus on developing first. Let's talk about how to increase your self-worth and identify some ways you can leverage it to be your best asset.

LEARNING TO SELF-VALUE

In this book, we've discussed a number of factors at work that are outside our control. But one of the most important factors for success is something we *can* control: how we see and value ourselves. You see, before we can expect others to value our contributions, we must value ourselves. And because, as POC, our experiences and perspectives likely differ from those of our colleagues, it's easy to think that our contributions are worth less than theirs simply because they're different. Even though the opposite is true—our unique experiences make us invaluable—it's still a trap that's easy to fall into.

And it's a trap that you—and you alone—can choose to avoid.

When was the last time you chose not to share an idea or ask a question during a meeting simply because you thought it wasn't good enough or smart enough? When was the last time you began a sentence with: "Sorry if this is a dumb question, but . . ."? If you're like most of us, you've done both pretty recently. But who told you your idea wasn't valid? Who told you to hold back and not contribute? Who told you your question was a dumb one? The answer to those questions is *you*—it's *you* who is holding yourself back.

In his theory, Rogers points out that much of how we value ourselves stems from external validation, but much of it also comes from within us. And although it isn't easy, if you're going to stop holding yourself back and be your true, open, and honest self at work, you must build the confidence to do so. That starts by learning to validate yourself, rather than looking for external validation.

I'm not saying that external validation isn't important, it absolutely is. It's a critical means of gathering positive feedback about the work we do (without our manager's feedback, how can we drive our careers forward?), and it's integral to building self-confidence. But it's also something outside of our control. Some managers are more adept at giving positive feedback than others. Sometimes, your boss may be swamped, and she won't have time to praise you for your work.

Because there are so many variables in play, it doesn't do us good to chase external validation. This is a lesson I learned the hard way. I'd spend countless hours revising a presentation just because I feared my boss wouldn't be thrilled with it. I'd second-guess myself over and over and tweak the deck endlessly (probably making it worse in the process), rather than just sending the version I was initially happy with. I naturally wanted my boss to be pleased and to note the hard work I'd put in, but I was also devaluing my own work and judgment by trying to read his mind and make the deck I thought *he'd* want rather than the deck I thought would be most effective for the client. Once I eventually realized that my need for external validation was having a negative impact on my work and my well-being, I was able to take a step back and learn to value my work on its own merits. I'd like to help you do the same.

We can't control the flow of external validation, so we have to resign ourselves to enjoying it when it happens and not despairing when it doesn't. After all, the absence of positive feedback does not mean you haven't done good work. So it's up to us to build confidence in our own abilities. The best way to do that is through self-validation.

UNDERSTAND YOUR NEED FOR EXTERNAL VALIDATION

At this point, I'm going to ask you to do something that will probably be a little uncomfortable. But as we've discussed throughout this book, allowing yourself to be uncomfortable can be a major catalyst for positive change. The next time you turn in a deliverable and crave positive external validation, I want you to ask yourself the following:

What do I hope this person says about what I just delivered? It's perfectly normal to want our work to be praised. We all want to do good work and be recognized for it. But as I've said, even if the person reviewing your work thinks it's terrific, they may not have the time or temperament to provide effusive praise. With this in mind, write out exactly what, in your ideal scenario, this person would say about your work.

Do I need this feedback, or do I just want it? Sometimes you need feedback to do your job or to perform better in the future. You may, for example, need feedback from a stakeholder before you can hand something off to another stakeholder or a client. If you don't need this feedback to function, however, ask yourself the next question.

Why do I want this feedback? Is it because you don't feel confident in your work? Do you want this person to like or respect you (or both)? Do you actually need it in order to perform better in the future?

What will happen if I don't receive the desired feedback—or any feedback at all? If you don't receive the desired feedback, what real-world consequences will occur? Will anything happen at all? Will your job be impacted in any way? In almost every case, the answer is no.

Now, let's consider a possible scenario. Imagine you've just handed a presentation to your manager for her to review before you present it to key stakeholders at a major account, and you've answered the questions as follows:

What do I hope this person says about what I just delivered? I hope she tells me that my work here is exceptional. I want her to be impressed by the amount of effort and thoughtfulness I've put into this, and I want her to tell me that I understand the client's challenge and have a clear plan for helping them overcome those challenges.

Do I need this feedback, or do I just want it? It would be helpful for future presentations, but not necessary. I really just want it.

Why do I want this feedback? Because I want to know that my contribution is acknowledged, and I want my boss to see me as someone who can carry the ball in key situations.

What will happen if I don't receive the desired feedback—or any feedback at all? Ultimately, nothing. I'll be a little disappointed, but my ability to do my job and my job security itself won't be impacted.

Let's imagine that your manager gave your presentation mixed reviews. She sent you an email saying: "This is a good first pass, and I can tell you swung for the fences on it. But you mention a use case for our solution that involves Oracle, and I recently learned that Oracle's newest marketing director just came from the company in the study you cite. It's probably not a great idea to mention them. Can you find a different use case to highlight? Also, you misspelled the CMO's last name on slide 39. Please fix. Thanks!"

That's mostly positive, right? She clearly acknowledges the level of effort and your willingness to go above and beyond. She also has inside knowledge to which you don't have access. Finally, she highlights a small but important error you made.

You could get discouraged here, but you have no real reason to. Of the two points she asks you to address, one is based on knowledge you didn't have at the time, so you can't reasonably be held accountable for it. The misspelling is a small error, and you have the opportunity to fix it before presenting it to the client. And you learned something: before presenting to a new client group, check the relevant stakeholders' LinkedIn accounts for clues about what you should and should not mention.

While your manager didn't rave about your work on the presentation, you should have no reason to be unhappy. It's easy to beat yourself up about this sort of thing, but don't. It's not productive or healthy, and it won't help you get ahead. What's more important is learning to give yourself the feedback you wanted from your manager. So let's learn how to do that.

GIVE YOURSELF THE CREDIT YOU DESERVE

When a friend or colleague has asked you to review their work because they were unsure about its quality, I'm sure you've told them their work was great, but they remained unconvinced. And when you've asked a peer for feedback on work you thought wasn't up to snuff, they've told you your work was terrific. We're our own worst critics, and it's easy for us to magnify even the tiniest flaws—whether real or perceived—in our own work. We judge ourselves far more harshly than we judge others, and that's often why we crave external validation. So before we can truly validate ourselves, we've got to learn to release our self-judgment. To do that, we've got to understand where it comes from.

Again, we look to Carl Rogers. He believed that parents place "conditions of worth" on their children, meaning that children feel affection and acceptance when they meet certain criteria.[60] For example, if a parent withholds affection from a child who has failed to earn an A on a test or has struck out in a Little League game, that child develops the subconscious notion that their worth as a person comes from delivering value of some kind.

Most of us carry these notions with us into adulthood. And in our adult lives, our managers and executives psychologically replace—or at least serve as a proxy for—our parents. In childhood, we rely on our parents to provide literally everything, from food to shelter to love. So it's normal for us to want to please our parents. As professionals, we rely on our jobs for the income that enables us to pay for the things we need in order to survive and thrive, and our managers have the most direct control over our continued employment. So just as we want to please our parents, we're heavily invested in making sure our work leaders are pleased with our progress.

Obviously, making sure our managers recognize and value our contributions is critical to continued success. But when we rely solely on their positive feedback in order to value our work, not only are we always held hostage by that need, we're also more prone to judge ourselves unnecessarily harshly. This prevents us from having the necessary confidence to volunteer for leadership initiatives or even just experiment with something new. That's why we must learn how to give ourselves *unconditional positive regard.*

That's what Rogers said therapists need to provide their patients in order to help them overcome the lasting negative effects of parental or employer conditions of worth.[61] In a nutshell, unconditional positive regard is the therapeutic practice of accepting and supporting an individual, regardless of what that person does, says, or believes. Providing this kind of support, Rogers believed, would help patients begin to see their own intrinsic value and enable them to begin overcoming anxiety, self-doubt, and depression.

For our purposes, learning to give ourselves unconditional positive regard will help us place more value on ourselves and our work. And, when practiced mindfully, it can also help us to be more accepting of others and their ideas and viewpoints.

To learn more about how to give ourselves unconditional positive regard, I spoke with Dr. Mark Sehl, a psychoanalyst who's been practicing in New York City for more than thirty-five years.

"There's no 'trick' to this," Dr. Sehl said. "There's no 'trick' to anything in psychology. Instead, it's all about being mindful and listening without judgment. You have to consciously remind yourself that you place no conditions on the patient. There's nothing they need to do to gain my approval. Their experiences and perspectives are valid and valuable just because they're human."

To apply those principles to ourselves, Dr. Sehl advocated taking the same approach. "Again, this is about two things: being mindful and remaining present," he said. "People are rarely present in the moment because they're worrying about the future, and they're thinking about failures in the past. But if you can stay in the moment and be aware of when you're experiencing self-judgment or self-doubt, you can eventually learn to overcome them. Be curious about the judgments you have about yourself and why you have them."

So when you experience these moments, take a step back and examine what you're feeling and why you're feeling it. The next time you find yourself criticizing yourself or your work, try this mindfulness exercise:

What am I feeling about myself in this moment? Your answer, for example, might be, "I feel inadequate" or "I'm afraid I may have disappointed my manager."

What am I feeling about my work in this moment? For example, "I fear my work isn't as good as that of my colleagues" or "I worry that I'll be fired."

Have I had these same feelings before? This could be, "Yes, the last time I had to present a deck to leadership."

What was the outcome the last time I had these feelings? Your answer might be, "The presentation went well" or "My manager had a few constructive notes, but overall, it was really positive."

Did my prejudgment of myself match the results, or did what I feared would happen actually occur? Very likely, your answer will be, "No, I did well in my presentation" or "No, my work was praised by multiple people."

If the answer to the previous question was no, why am I still judging myself? You may answer, "I can't get over the fear of failure" or "I really want my manager to give more effusive praise."

As Dr. Sehl noted, doing this exercise once, twice, or even three times will do you very little good. Learning to readily self-validate requires practice over time. Some can accomplish it in months; for others, it will take years. You can't change your thoughts and feelings overnight, but by being aware of moments of self-judgment and self-doubt and practicing these mindfulness exercises, you'll chip away at the kind of negative thinking that can hold you back at work and keep you from being your truest, best self.

How to Stay True to Your Best Self at Work

Learning to be your best self takes practice, mindfulness, and being present. Staying true to who you are is no different. So many factors can impact how we see ourselves, what we value, and how we interact with others. But now that we've learned how to identify our best selves and ways to proactively care for ourselves, let's talk about ways to ensure we don't let ourselves be compromised by external factors.

Our selves are malleable. You're not the same person today that you were five years ago. You've learned and experienced new things that have changed your worldview. You've been exposed to different viewpoints that have shaped your values and opinions. And you may even have compromised a value in order to fit in at work or get ahead.

Most of these changes are great. It's how you grow, after all. That last one, however, isn't.

When we compromise ourselves, we give a bit of ourselves away. We can lose sight of the values, viewpoints, and experiences that make us who we are. And when you do that often enough, it can eventually be hard to recognize yourself, let alone be your best self.

As POC, what makes us who we are is also what makes us such valuable resources for our employers. If we compromise these things, we're not only betraying ourselves, we're short changing our employers. But in a working world dominated by majority professionals, it can be extremely difficult to stay true to ourselves when the culture we're surrounded by doesn't fully align with our own.

YOUR INNER AND OUTER LAYERS

Think about the structure of a basketball. There's the outer layer of leather that you touch and interact with, as well as the air inside it. Without the air to keep the ball inflated, the outer layer is essentially useless. And if the outer layer is punctured, it deflates quickly. Both parts have to remain complete in order for the ball to be effective. The ball's surface changes over time through wear and use, and the air inside has to be regularly replenished.

I think of selfhood in a similar fashion. Our external selves—aspects that others see and interact with on a daily basis—can and do change over time. We can change how we act, what we say, and how we interact with others. We also become worn down. Our inner selves, however, are invisible to others and must be regularly replenished through introspection, learning, personal growth, and remaining true to our values. Both layers must be whole for us to be our fullest selves.

ON THE SURFACE

Like the ball's surface, your outermost layer is the most changeable. It's the layer that comes into contact with other people and reacts to the things they do and say. If, for example, your significant other says you look good in a certain color, you'll probably wear that color more often. If your boss asks you to come in earlier, you'll adjust your schedule. Think of your outermost layer like the clothes you put on every day. They change according to the weather, the occasion, or even your mood.

Your outermost layer is the one people see. It's the one to which they react and, unfortunately, use to judge. For POC, this often means being cautious about how this layer appears to our colleagues—including how we look, how we act, what we say, and even how we sound. This is a reason so many POC engage in what's known as "code-switching": adopting the culture, customs, and vernacular of a majority culture. If, for example, you speak one way to your friends and family and another way to coworkers, you're code-switching.

There are a number of reasons people code-switch. Sometimes we do it—even unconsciously—because we want to fit in. Sometimes we do it because we fear that how we look or speak will result in negative judgment from our peers. Some may do it because they see it as the path of least resistance and a faster way to get ahead.

Your ability to opt out of code-switching will largely depend on the degree you're comfortable being yourself around colleagues. It's easy when we're comfortable, but when we're uncertain, it can feel risky. Yet, as we've discussed many times, being willing to take risks and accept being uncomfortable is critical to doing your best work.

Another important component of your self's surface layer is your set of boundaries. These are the limits of your personal and professional comfort zone, and they define the terms on which you interact with others—and allow others to interact with you. Like everything on the surface, your boundaries may change quickly. You may be hesitant to share information about your personal life, like your favorite music or the movies you like, with your colleagues. You may also feel uncomfortable inviting coworkers out for coffee or a drink after work.

But as you become more comfortable using mindfulness to identify why a self-judgment holds you back from being who you are at work, these boundaries can and likely will change. Examine your existing boundaries and determine which you're willing to expand by completing this simple exercise. Consider the six personal and professional boundaries listed, and check the box that most accurately represents how often or how willing you are to do each.

MY PERSONAL AND PROFESSIONAL BOUNDARIES	ALWAYS	SOMETIMES	NEVER
I share my hobbies and personal interests with at least some of my coworkers.			
I feel comfortable engaging with them in events outside of work.			
I'm capable of being vulnerable and asking for help when I need it.			
I'm comfortable giving constructive feedback to my peers.			
I can receive constructive feedback without becoming defensive or resentful.			
I'm willing to work on nights and weekends to achieve my goals or help my company be successful.			

Now take a moment to examine your answers. For example, if you never share your hobbies and interests at work, try describing why you don't.

If you answered "always" or "sometimes" more often than not, it's likely that your boundaries are generally open and flexible. Conversely, if most of your answers are "never," then you likely have very finite and limited boundaries. This is a sign that you don't feel comfortable being who you are at work. If that's the case, challenge yourself a bit. Choose one of the behaviors you answered with "never" and try to do the opposite the next time you're in the office and the opportunity arises. Let's say you said you're never comfortable with feeling vulnerable and asking for help. The next time you truly need help with something, try asking for it. Take a chance and be mindful of how the person you asked for assistance reacts and how you feel in the moment, both when asking and when that person offers to assist. (In my experience, people are generally happy to help.)

WHAT LIES BENEATH

Even though it's both invisible and intangible, the air inside a basketball makes up the majority of the ball itself. So, too, do our inner selves constitute the vast majority of what makes us who we are. Our thoughts, feelings, and values may be inaccessible to others, but they underpin the parts of ourselves we share with others. To share effectively, we have to replenish our inner selves regularly—and ensure that we don't allow parts of it to slip away.

To replenish yourself, you need to step outside of your comfort zone and push yourself to grow as a person and as a professional. Complacency, while comfortable, is a dangerous state of being. You probably recognize this behavior in some of your disengaged coworkers: they show up, clock in, and zone out. They do the bare minimum required to keep their jobs—and if they continue that way, it's unlikely they'll ever get ahead. If you're reading this book, it's safe to assume that you're an ambitious person who wants to better yourself and grow your career. You may be thinking, *That could never happen to me*. But I assure you, it can. Inertia is a powerful thing. A few setbacks in a career, like a poor relationship with your manager or getting passed over for a promotion, can cause even the most ambitious among us to just give up and settle for *good enough*.

The mindfulness exercises we've laid out in this chapter can go a long way in validating yourself and your work, and that's critical for counteracting inertia and remaining engaged—but it's not enough. You have to replenish your energy and interest in your work by actively investing in it. Challenge yourself to read a career book every month. Give yourself a goal of attending a networking event once a month. Dedicate some of the time you might otherwise spend watching TV or browsing social media to listening to a podcast or a lecture that makes you better at your job. Ask your mentor for guidance on other ways you can improve and grow.

If keeping yourself intellectually engaged with your career is the best way to pump fresh air into your ball, the best way to keep it there is by staying true to yourself and your values.

Every time you allow one of your core values to be compromised, you're giving a little bit of yourself away. Let's say you're a sales rep for a software company. You always hit your quota, but you're always trailing the top performer on the team. You ask your manager if it would be okay if you shadowed him on a few sales calls so you can learn and find ways to improve. But as you listen to him speak to prospects, you learn that he repeatedly promises access to functionality that doesn't exist—and isn't coming any time soon. When you ask him about this tactic, he tells you it's his secret weapon. After all, he says, they're signing a twelve-month contract, and we can always tell them those features hit a delay in development.

What would you do? You can use the tactic yourself, if you want. It'll make your numbers go up, and your boss will be happy. But it's also dishonest, unethical, and bad for your company in the long run, since that client will likely be disappointed and opt out of their contract as soon as they can. If you consider honesty and transparency core values, could you live with yourself if you chose to follow his advice? Would you feel as if you were doing good work every day and being your best, truest self at work? I doubt it, and that's exactly what I'm talking about here. Staying true to yourself isn't something you do passively. It requires attention, energy, and proactivity. If you don't commit to those, inertia and complacency can take over, and your career will stall—possibly for good.

How to Talk about Politics at Work

First things first: we're not going to talk about *whether* you should talk about politics at work. We're going to talk about *how* to talk about politics when it comes up—because it will come up. In today's divisive, emotionally charged political climate, talking politics in the office is inevitable. When done right, it can provide catharsis and bring you closer to your coworkers. When done wrong, however, it may change how you and your colleagues feel about each other. It may get you in trouble—or even fired. So let's find a way to bring your political self to the office in a way that doesn't stifle debate, create division, or have negative consequences for your career.

UNDERSTAND YOUR COMPANY'S CULTURE WHEN IT COMES TO POLITICS

Perhaps your workplace officially frowns on political discussions on the job; inevitably, those conversations happen anyway, but they may take place furtively or on lunch hours. After all, it's not as though you can leave a major portion of you who are you at the door at 9 a.m. and pick it back up again at 6 p.m. Being able to bring every part of yourself to work will help create a much more inclusive environment for everyone—but when it comes to politics, there's a measure of risk involved. That's why it's critical that you understand your company's culture and its attitude toward politics in the workplace.

Start by reviewing your company's employee handbook, if one is available. It may provide guidance for what is and is not acceptable to discuss at work. But even if it doesn't, you should always know your rights as an employee in the state in which you work. In many states, private companies have the right to terminate people for taking overt political stances. In my experience, instances of companies doing so are rare, but it is possible. The much more likely scenario is a mandatory meeting with your manager or possibly human resources.

So now we see the problem: political discussions will arise—and that's a good thing. But there may be consequences if you're not mindful about how you conduct yourself during these discussions.

DON'T RUSH TO JUDGMENT

When someone holds an opposing viewpoint on a political issue, we may make immediate assumptions about other views they hold—but we've discussed all the very good reasons that making assumptions is never wise or correct. For example, when you learn that a coworker opposes gun control, you may unconsciously assume that she holds other views commonly associated with others who also oppose gun control. But allowing yourself to engage in that type of thinking can be dangerous. You may make automatic judgments about her values, beliefs, and background that can lead to animosity or even overt anger—even though you don't actually know how she feels about any of those other issues.

Instead of judging, seek to understand why your coworker feels the way she does about a particular topic. Even though you may disagree with her, it's still worth trying to learn why she feels the way she does. You might discover that her lived experience has influenced her view on a topic in a way that might not have occurred to you. Instead of rushing to judgment, start by asking questions. Which leads me to my next point.

USE THE SOCRATIC METHOD

Think about a completely pointless argument about politics that you've witnessed, in which both parties are shouting over each other, citing sound bites and talking points, even resorting to name calling. Maybe it happened in school or with friends or at a family get-together. These arguments accomplish nothing, aside from raising the participants' blood pressures and potentially souring once-close relationships. In fact, a study by corporate communication and leadership training firm VitalSmarts found that during the 2016 presidential election, one out of three people surveyed reported being attacked, insulted, or called names. A quarter also said political arguments had hurt a relationship.[62]

The problem here is not that people disagree with each other; it's that they're just arguing instead of seeking to understand one another. That's the worst way to discuss politics (or anything, really). The best way, however, isn't an argument at all.

It's called the Socratic method. Named for the ancient Greek philosopher Socrates, this method is designed to surface implicit biases, develop understanding, and craft logical refutations of illogical answers. Rather than both sides arguing contradicting viewpoints, it involves one party asking simple, objective questions to establish what is true and what isn't. It's a lot like a cross-examination in a court of law. One person asks, the other person answers, and neither person injects personal feelings into either questions or answers. It's strictly factual, and that's perfect for a workplace setting, as it helps avoid creating the kind of tension that causes tempers to flare.

So how does it work exactly? Well, the noted philosopher Richard W. Paul posited that one can employ six types of questions within the Socratic method.

Questions for clarification: "What do you mean by that?" or "How does this relate to the discussion we're having?"

Questions that probe assumptions: "Why do you assume left-handed pitchers are more desirable?" or "What leads you to believe that CNN is an untrustworthy news source?"

Questions that probe reasons and evidence: "What proof do you have that the government faked the moon landing?" or "Can you provide evidence that proves that Stephen Curry is objectively better than LeBron James?"

Questions about viewpoints and perspectives: "Can we look at this problem from another angle?" or "What do you think an expert in the field might say to that answer?"

Questions that probe implications and consequences: "What would the consequences be if that statement were true?" or "Are you implying something with your last answer?"

Questions about the question: "Why do you think I asked that question?" or "When you say 'best,' how are you defining that word?"

Note that nowhere in these examples are we discussing what we feel, think, or believe. We're not inserting ourselves in here at all—we're simply asking direct, simple questions. No opinions are involved. And since the questions are simple, direct, and without opinion, we can use them to foster constructive political discourse with our colleagues while remaining dispassionate and rational. Let's look at two examples.

SCENARIO ONE

Imagine that your coworker Scott reacts to a news article he's just read about a newly proposed gun control measure that seeks to ban assault rifles.

"Love how the government wants to prevent us from keeping ourselves safe," he states to the team.

You might be tempted to argue, but the better move here would be to ask a simple, direct question:

"How would a ban on assault rifles prevent you from keeping yourself safe?"

Scott tells you that even though he now lives in a major city, he grew up in a very rural farming community, and when law enforcement officers were available, they were likely twenty to thirty minutes away at best. Therefore, home protection was largely do-it-yourself for most households.

That, I think, is a fair point, but you have the opportunity to add nuance and seek common ground here by asking a few more questions:

"How do you define 'safe'?"

"Well," he says, "I think it would be the ability to deter or prevent an armed intruder from harming my family or me."

Now you have the opportunity to ask Scott another question:

"Would a hunting rifle or handgun make you objectively less capable of doing that than an assault rifle would?"

Scott concedes that no, they wouldn't make a household any less safe.

See what happened there? First, we engaged Scott in a way that didn't make him feel defensive about his viewpoints. Instead of saying something incendiary like, "Oh, I guess you don't notice all these kids getting shot at school, huh?" you merely asked a series of calm, factual questions that had simple, logical answers. Second, you got Scott to think differently about an issue—and that's enough for now. It's crucial not to use this method to attempt to force your coworkers to see political issues the same way you do. Getting Scott to examine a different point of view is in itself an accomplishment.

If gun violence or assault rifles comes up again at work, you can begin again, starting from where you left off. Do *not* continue questioning to the point that your coworker becomes frustrated or angry. Small steps lead to bigger outcomes here.

SCENARIO TWO

Katie loves the U.S. president currently in office. Unlike Scott, who rarely discusses politics, Katie voices her support for the president loudly and often. Engaging her in a political discussion is going to be a little more challenging than doing so with Scott. In her case, it's best to do it in even smaller chunks that focus on enabling her to draw her own conclusions based on research.

One day, Katie says to your team: "I wish the media would stop making it seem like the president's not doing a good job."

You can respond with: "What are they reporting that makes you think that's the case?"

"The president said that ICE has liberated towns from being controlled by MS-13," Katie says, "but the *New York Times* said that's not true."

"Why do they say it's not true?" you ask.

"They said he doesn't have any proof."

"Does he?" you ask again.

"I don't know," she answers. "He must; otherwise, he wouldn't have said anything."

Now, at this point, you can choose one of two possible options based on Katie's level of frustration. If she seems angry or tense, then pause the discussion. After all, you've already gotten Katie to consciously admit that it's possible the media aren't lying. But if she isn't getting heated, you can go one—and only one—level deeper.

"Do politicians and elected officials always tell the truth?" you ask.

"No! Of course not!"

"So, is it fair to say that it's possible he's lying or at least exaggerating?"

No matter how Katie responds to this, you're done for the day. Continuing will wear her out and make her resentful, and that's no good for anyone.

We've used the Socratic method to encourage Katie to step outside of what she accepts as fundamentally true and to question whether there may be another point to consider. And—this is key—at no point during either exchange described here did I use the word "I." Equally important, I didn't try to convince anyone to change either colleague's position or question their beliefs by emphasizing facts and statistics. Because—surprisingly—that just doesn't work. At all.

Confirmation Bias

You might think that showing someone a set of established facts or a scientific consensus that disproves or at least challenges their beliefs would be effective. I mean, these are facts, right? But amazingly, it not only doesn't work, but it can actually strengthen their beliefs and make them even more convinced that they're correct. A number of studies show this to be true, and there are theories as to why it happens, but the consensus is that it is true.

One possible reason is what's known as "confirmation bias." Elizabeth Kolbert sums this up perfectly in a *New Yorker* article entitled "Why Facts Don't Change Our Minds."[63] Among other studies, she described a Stanford research project with two groups of students: one group was opposed to capital punishment and believed it did nothing to deter crime, and the other believed just the opposite. Here's what happened:

The students were asked to respond to two studies. One provided evidence in support of the deterrence argument, and the other offered data that called it into question. Both studies—you guessed it—were made up; they were designed to present what were, objectively speaking, equally compelling statistics. The students who had originally supported capital punishment rated the pro-deterrence data highly credible and the anti-deterrence data unconvincing; the students who opposed capital punishment did the reverse. At the end of the experiment, the students were once again asked about their views. Those who'd started out pro-capital punishment were now even more in favor of it; those who'd opposed it were even more resolute.

It seems that many of us don't like being shown facts that challenge our beliefs, and we react by doubling down on those beliefs rather than questioning them. So instead of trying to get a coworker to alter a deeply held belief, simply ask questions that can lead them to do their own research.

ADDITIONAL THOUGHTS AND BEST PRACTICES

Following are a few more things to keep in mind about discussing politics at work.

Keep it among your peers. Don't talk politics with your manager. Ever. Even if the two of you enjoy a close, trusting relationship and you think you know where she leans politically, it's not worth the risk. And if you're a manager, don't discuss politics with your direct reports—it could give them the impression that there will be repercussions if they take a stance that runs counter to yours. In all instances, keep it to your current professional level.

Don't let your guard down. Staying late at the office? Having drinks or dinner after a long workday? Great—enjoy it. But don't let a casual setting lull you into oversharing. If the conversation turns to politics, remember the Socratic method, or better yet, change the subject altogether.

Never, ever discuss politics with a client or a prospect. If you're in sales, account management, or any other client-facing role, resist the urge to discuss politics (or anything potentially sensitive) with clients or would-be clients. Even if they bring it up—and even if agreeing and being chummy feels as if it might help close the deal—keep it strictly professional. You run the risk of costing your company the sale or losing an existing client, and it's not worth it. If a client mentions something political, simply say, "Yeah, I hear you," and change the subject.

In this chapter, I hope I've made a persuasive case for the value of introspection, mindfulness, and self-validation. I hope you've learned some tactics you can use to better yourself and stay true to what you value and believe in. I also hope you've gained some tools for discussing politics at work in a way that won't cause division between you and coworkers. All in all, this chapter should help you bring your entire, authentic self to work every day.

Now it's time to use your best self to build tomorrow's diverse workforce today.

A TIME TO LEAD

7

LEADING THE CHANGE

A Proactive Approach to Building a More Diverse and Inclusive Workforce

Now that you have a plan for continued success and growth, it's time to take the next step in your career: becoming a leader. And there's no greater opportunity to make an impact than by taking the lead on building a more diverse workforce.

POC have yet another unique opportunity here for many of the reasons we've already discussed and one we haven't: expertise. We inherently have more expertise in building more diverse and inclusive workplaces, simply by virtue of belonging to one of these communities. And we have a higher level of credibility, given our personal experiences. Members of our communities are more inclined to trust us, and we're better able to tailor recruiting messages for them.

This does not obviate the need for traditional allies. As we'll see in this chapter and the next, with the power that they've enjoyed to date, some of your majority colleagues can be instrumental in making sure the right people are listening at the highest levels of your organization. First, at the executive level, they can provide sponsorship, exert influence, and help create buy-in across the organization. Second, a truly inclusive organization means participation by all groups, including the majority.

But before we go any further, let me be clear: this is going to be challenging.

Making diversity a priority means heightened visibility as you undertake difficult conversations with coworkers and managers. Some will disagree with you, perhaps even vehemently. Others will dismiss it as "not a real business problem." A few might view it as a cynical exercise in self-promotion. But if this book has shown you just one thing, I hope it's that workplace diversity has measurable business benefits and should be a top priority for companies who want to stay competitive in the years to come. And, as this country moves toward a diverse majority in the next twenty years, it's critical—for both workers and employers—that we set the stage for open and diverse workplaces now. In the case of the American professionals of color, the right initiatives put in place now will pave the way for more management and executive opportunities in the coming decades. For current employers, it's a chance to attract and retain the best talent before it's drawn elsewhere.

In this chapter, we'll discuss ways in which you can begin making a visible difference in the culture of diversity and inclusion at your organization. Some changes will be small and personal; others will have more far-reaching consequences. With each step you take, you'll be closer to assuming the mantle of your organization's diversity champion.

But keep in mind that when we talk about diversity and inclusion initiatives, we're talking about more than the distribution of POC on staff and in management. Achieving a truly diverse and inclusive workplace requires diversity of *everyone*, regardless of ethnicity or gender. While POC can take the lead, for this to have a meaningful effect, everyone must be invested and given a seat at the table.

Human resources consultants Gardenswartz and Rowe recommend thinking about diversity as layers of traits, some of which are in our control and some of which are not. The centermost layer is the personality—the individual characteristics that inform our behavior. Next are internal dimensions, which are aspects we can't control, such as gender and age. The third layer, external dimensions, includes traits such as education and appearance. Finally, the fourth layer, organizational dimensions, includes the things employers control, such as work location and department assignment.[64] Creating a more diverse workplace means everyone—regardless of ethnicity and gender—must buy in and participate actively.

My point is this: if our goal is to create an inclusive, diverse, and vibrant workforce, it can't just mean inclusive of POC. It must mean inclusive of all people, in all their diversity. In the workplace of the future, everyone should get an equal voice and equal representation.

The Dawn of the Diversity Champion

If the era of hashtag activism has taught us anything, it's that there's power in the masses. Change happens when a critical mass of people gathers behind a cause or issue. In recent years, marches, rallies, and demonstrations have been the markers of change, or at least of the desire for change. So you may wonder what, if anything, the lone individual can accomplish.

Frankly, it depends on the individual. For real change to take place, you must be willing to put in the work and make a convincing case for your vision. After that, you have to follow through, building trust with employees, organizing other individuals, and executing on your plan. Finally, you need to review and measure your results and then reiterate your actions. Championing a cause, especially among the colleagues and friends you work with every day, is not for the faint of heart. But someone needs to take up the cause.

Here's how.

What Is a Diversity Champion?

More than a human resources watchdog, more than a committee head, a diversity champion is the driving force behind culture change at an organization. Part educator, part facilitator, part active listener, the diversity champion assesses needs, leads conversations, and organizes events focused on creating a more inclusive workplace environment.

The diversity champion must be able to understand the nuanced and sensitive nature of conversations on this subject matter and issues of change management in general. The champion might come from a management or nonmanagement position, but in the latter case should make it a priority to gain managerial buy-in as soon as possible. That kind of support will help ensure knowledge transfer and participation across departments and divisions.

Most important, the diversity champion ensures that "diversity" isn't just a buzzword reserved for job descriptions and About Us pages, or, as writer and Jezebel founder Anna Holmes put it in *The New York Times Magazine*, "both euphemism and cliché, [it's] a convenient shorthand that gestures at inclusivity and representation without actually taking them seriously."[65]

Much of what's written about diversity champions focuses on the CEO and her responsibility in engaging employees in culture change. And while it's true that certain changes require top-down initiative, I don't believe that significant culture shifts are the exclusive purview of the corner office. In fact, with a certain level of executive or managerial buy-in, I think a grassroots effort led by a diverse group of passionate employees can lead to broader, more lasting change.

BAND TOGETHER

Imagine that a technology company has 500 employees and 15 are Black (3%), 20 are Latinx or Hispanic (5%), and 5 are Native American (1%). How much impact on recruiting do you think 15 employees could have? The answer is, of course, very little. What could happen if we tripled those numbers? If all the Black, Latinx and Hispanic, and Native American employees were to work together, they'd be one-tenth of the company's workforce and would have more influence than several smaller communities. None of us likes to be lumped into groups by our peers. But in this case, we're the ones doing the bundling, which is okay because who knows more than we do about the challenges POC face in the workplace?

Becoming a Diversity Champion

If you don't think you're quite ready to take on the role of diversity champion, there's no need to rush. This is something you can grow into, and there are many challenges to tackle in the office setting. Start small—begin with things you can do, such as changes to your own attitude and behavior, and slowly expand those actions. Once you earn trust and buy-in from your peers, you'll be in a better position to approach management with broader goals.

Before you can begin to create change at your organization, however, you may first need to make changes within yourself.

CHAMPION, KNOW THYSELF

We've already talked at length about the importance of staying true to yourself, and the dangers of biases both explicit and implicit.

When it comes to advocacy, it can be all too easy to put on the social justice blinders and forget about your own weaknesses. Now, I'm not saying you have to model perfect inclusive behavior before you can become a diversity champion. There is no such thing. I am saying that it's critical to be self-aware; when you can recognize your own shortcomings, it's easier to empathize with others', and that spurs honest conversation. Before you ask others to change, ask yourself some key questions.

AM I CULTURALLY COMPETENT?

You may be in touch with your own roots—that may be what's spurring you on to create change within your organization—but a diverse organization doesn't just mean representation of many cultures. It means active acceptance, engagement, and participation *across* those cultures. So talk to your colleagues. Find out who they are, the traditions in which they've been steeped, and how those traditions shaped them.

DO I ENGAGE IN INSENSITIVE BEHAVIOR?

Unless you walk the walk, don't expect others to trust you when you talk the talk. It doesn't take a microaggression to make someone feel excluded. Whether you intend it or not, certain behavior—like frequent interruption or lack of eye contact—can marginalize team members, some of whom are already dealing with marginalization every day.

DO I ACTIVELY LISTEN TO OTHERS?

This isn't just about understanding other cultures. No lone champion, no matter how big her cape, can create change all by herself. You might as well know before you start down this path: you're going to need more than one brain on this. If you're not already engaging with your colleagues, start now. It doesn't have to be a formal interview or even diversity- and inclusion-related. Grab a coffee with the new person, attend that happy hour you were planning on skipping, join a cross-functional committee. The point is to get in the habit of listening to others before you begin to speak for them.

We all fall short in these areas from time to time. Perfect behavior is not the goal here. The key hallmarks of the diversity champion, rather, are self-awareness and willingness to change, to listen to others, and to lead others in creating change. If you can commit to those, you've already completed a significant step.

The next step, however, is more difficult. It's time to take action.

Create a Foundation for Change

Creating change, whether personal, professional, or organizational, can be overwhelming, even terrifying. It's not just the risk of failure; it's not knowing where to even begin. But at the end of the day, the big changes we seek are nothing more than a collection of small changes. Or, as Vincent van Gogh said much more articulately: "Great things are not done by impulse, but by a series of small things brought together."

When faced with a big problem—something as endemic as, say, bias in your workplace—it's best to start with one small, easy change. This may be something that in the long run has no greater consequence than simply getting you off the ground and moving. There are many small ways in which you can nurture change at your organization. Sooner or later those small steps accumulate, until you not only have the foundation for a real culture shift but have also earned trust and buy-in from colleagues and managers. And that will pave the way for you to assume a more formal leadership role in promoting change across the enterprise.

Here are a few small (and not-so-small) ways to start.

RESEARCH EXISTING POLICIES AND PROGRAMS

Before you go banging on doors and talking about change, make a good faith effort to understand the policies and programs your organization already has on the books, and how, if at all, those are executed on. Get familiar with your employee handbook and company website. Make friends with your human resources representative. Check internal blogs or your intranet for event postings. You're looking not just for formal policy, but for any guidelines for how to behave around your colleagues. That includes how meetings are conducted, how administrative work is divided up, even something as small as who gets to choose lunch when. An inclusive organization creates openness across all areas.

Finally, be sure to speak with colleagues of color who have been at your company for a year or more. Have the company's policies made them feel included or excluded? Have diversity guidelines been acted on, or is follow-through lacking? The idea is not to cast blame or sow the seeds of discontent. Be clear that this is an opportunity to change things for the better, and as such, their constructive criticism is welcome.

DON'T JUDGE; CORRECT

If you're going to help create a more inclusive and diverse workplace, you'll need to be vigilant for signs and symptoms of bias or intolerance. But you'll also need to be understanding. As we've already discussed, most people who demonstrate implicit bias are not actually racist or intending to be hurtful. They may not realize that what they're doing is exclusionary; they may even think they're being complimentary.

It's important to correct their bias, but it's equally important to refrain from judging them. You don't know what prompted them to say what they said or act as they did, and assuming it comes from a place of intolerance or willful ignorance will serve only to alienate potential allies. Remember, true inclusion means that everyone has a seat at the table, regardless of whether they're in the majority or minority group.

When a majority- or minority-group colleague commits an act of implicit bias, gently point out that their assumption is just that, and if the bias is directed at your group or one you feel comfortable speaking for, use the opportunity to share some information. You're more likely to start a conversation—and conversations, not lectures, help change minds.

BE A BETTER MEETING HOST

Here's another example of how changing your behavior in a small way can lead to organization-wide shifts. Study after study has been conducted on effective and ineffective ways to conduct meetings. From power seating positions to timed topic discussions, meetings have been hacked in nearly every possible way.

Trends aside, there are some excellent techniques available to make sure your meetings are inclusive and benefit from the wisdom that diversity brings. The recruiting software firm Lever, whose staff boasts an impressive 50:50 ratio of men to women, published a fantastic list of more than fifty ways employees can promote diversity, three of which I've included, in their words:

> *Share discussion points and an agenda prior to meetings so more voices are heard. Some people like to talk through new information immediately, whereas others like to have time to process information. By presenting a problem on the spot, you're less likely to receive the latter group's contribution.*

> *Try the Round Robin technique in meetings, where you ask every person in the room for a contribution to the discussion at hand. People can either share an idea, or pass.*
>
> *Point out interruptions. Studies show that women are far more likely than men to be interrupted in meetings.*[66]

Again, this is not about shaming the person who interrupted or who dominated the conversation, but a gentle reminder and request to cede the floor back to others will help all members feel included and will lead to better ideas.

LEARN FROM OTHER ORGANIZATIONS

Much of what I write about in this book—much of the knowledge that Jopwell is founded on—has been synthesized from the successes and failures of other companies and the insights and expert advice of thought leaders in this space.

There is nothing wrong with taking what others have developed and incorporating it into your own plan for building diversity and inclusion. In fact, many of the companies that see success in this area publish case studies so that others can benefit, as do diversity-and-inclusion nonprofits and consultancies. At Jopwell, we write about success stories regularly in our blog's "From the Desk Of" series.

Leverage your network as another source of information. Talk to the people you know about what their organizations get right and wrong about diversity and inclusion. Whether you're scouring the web or talking to friends, try to answer the following questions, which will help you find examples that most closely resemble your own organization and its needs:

- How big is the organization?
- What, roughly, is the ratio of POC to majority employees?
- Are there particular groups that are very well represented?

- How long did it take to reach that ratio?
- What made the organization attractive to these groups?
- Did the organization engage in targeted recruitment efforts?
- Once hired, how were new POC employees brought into the cultural fold?
- Is there an official diversity and inclusion policy on the books, and how is it enforced?
- What programs does the organization run to encourage inclusion?
- Is inclusion a top-down (executive-driven) or bottom-up (employee-driven) effort?
- How supportive is management?
- How are diversity and inclusion efforts reflected in the company's day-to-day operations?
- How many vendors and suppliers are owned by women or minorities? Is this number intentional?

As you learn more about these other organizations, consider starting a "best practices" file, with categories for recruitment and retention, policy and procedure, culture, programming, executive buy-in, vendors, and suppliers. File the case studies with the most pertinent sections highlighted or summarized under the categories. You're essentially creating a diversity and inclusion playbook you can refer to over and over again—in conversations with human resources, with other interested colleagues, and with executives whose buy-in you seek (more on that later).

BECOME A MENTOR OR A REVERSE MENTOR

We've discussed the importance of working with a mentor and setting goals for your personal and professional development. If you've found success with your mentor, consider paying it forward by being a mentor, especially to new or other divers employees. Mentoring can help new employees adjust to organizational culture and find a place for themselves at a company. But you won't just be helping put them on the path to success; you may even change the demographics of management at your organization. A study published in *Financial Management* magazine found that mentored employees were promoted every 44.6 months, while nonmentored, but still high-performing, employees were promoted only every 59.4 months.[67]

Alternatively, talk to your human resources department about the opportunities for reverse mentoring—mentoring an older, more senior colleague. Reverse mentoring looks a lot like traditional mentoring, but with the roles, well, reversed. You'll provide advice and perspective on what it's like to be a young professional of color in your organization and out in the world. In doing so, you'll help bridge divides of generation, ethnicity, culture, gender, or more.

But what's the benefit to you? Reverse mentoring brings all the benefits of traditional mentoring—exposure to senior management, greater visibility, networking opportunities, and strategic career advice—with the added perk of putting you in a position to help change corporate culture. The rules of mentoring apply; you'll want to set goals on both sides, commit to a schedule, and focus on open, honest conversation. This is not a forum for you to badger your mentee about stereotypes; they're making a good faith effort here. Instead, come up with some topics of mutual interest that you can use to start a conversation about diversity and inclusion. Always educate, never berate.

If your organization doesn't have a formal mentoring or reverse mentoring program in place, talk to human resources about how you might start one up and ask them for help in approaching senior leadership.

PRACTICE ACTIVE LISTENING

Active listening doesn't come easily to many of us. Whether we agree or disagree with what's being said in a conversation, we often find ourselves merely waiting to talk while someone else is speaking. When we do this, not only are we not truly processing what's being said, we're signaling to the speaker that we're not all that interested in their point of view. When you're having conversations with your colleagues about their experiences and perspectives, it's important to practice active listening techniques. Here are a few tactics to use to make sure you're being an active listener:

Focus on what's being said. When you're listening to a conversation partner, don't think about what you're going to say next. Don't prepare a rejoinder. Don't think about how what they're saying relates (or doesn't!) to you. Just focus on what they're saying.

Repeat what they've said back to them. Say, "What I'm hearing you express is (and then paraphrasing their statement)," which is an effective way to both process and retain what they said and also signal to them that you're truly listening and taking it in.

Be mindful of your body language. Think about the conversations you've had with someone who either clearly wasn't listening or was obviously just preparing to disagree or pass judgment. They probably had their arms crossed, or their eyes were wandering. Maybe they just kept interrupting. When you're practicing active listening, maintain eye contact, nod occasionally, and don't cross your arms. Keep an open body posture and avoid sending negative signals, such as rolling your eyes or sighing.

JOIN AN EMPLOYEE RESOURCE GROUP

Sometimes called affinity groups or employee networks, employee resource groups (ERGs) are executive-sponsored, voluntary organizations of individuals within a company. Many ERGs comprise employees of a particular ethnic background, gender, orientation, generation, or other demographic variable. They're a safe space to meet like-minded colleagues, discuss issues that affect their members, and celebrate cultural values. Your company, for example, might have a Latinx ERG, a young professionals ERG, or an LGBTQ + ERG.

For the young professional, an ERG can be a great way to network within your organization, find solutions to challenges faced by your particular group, and take on new leadership opportunities. There's a lot of good work you can do in an ERG that will benefit both the members and the organization at large. For example, some companies work with ERGs to help improve recruitment, get a better look into their customer base, and serve as a sounding board for diversity councils. At Bloomberg, for example, ERGs—there called "communities"—host client events to help foster client relationships and drive sales, and help recruit minority, veteran, and female talent.[68]

But there's a catch. If your goal is to lead your organization into a more diverse and inclusive future, you may not want to put all your eggs in the ERG basket. Unless your ERG happens to be very diverse or has deep ties to executive-level diversity councils or initiatives, it can become an easy way to isolate yourself among members of your own group. And while this may feel safe and offers the advantages of congregating with people with a common background, it won't help you learn about or support other groups.

To do that, you'll need to branch out. Find ways to cosponsor events with other ERGs. Get in front of your organization's diversity council (if one exists) and advocate for cross-ERG cooperation. Or use your ERG as a sandbox for piloting new kinds of initiatives that can later be rolled out company wide. The point is, don't take your eye off the long-term prize: building an organizational culture that is inclusive and supportive of *all* employees.

The Next Step: Creating Company-Wide Initiatives

If the options I've just outlined seem small, be patient. Each of these is an entry point into the world of diversity and inclusion leadership. Use these steps to nurture the skills you'll need for your next move: building enterprise-level consensus for a diversity-and-inclusion initiative—namely, a D&I council. To be successful, you'll need to excel in communication, active listening, collaboration, planning, and logistics. You'll need to learn how to defend your point without becoming angry, how to be assertive and not aggressive, and how to navigate the choppy waters of this very sensitive topic while still making all parties, even majority parties, feel included. This is why I suggest you practice by engaging in the opportunities already discussed.

Challenges aside, what comes next can be an extremely positive experience for diversity champions. An organization-spanning council has the power to create real, lasting change—change that will pave the way for commercial success as it simultaneously creates a more attractive environment for new and existing employees. If you have the strength and stamina for it, you may never experience anything else quite as rewarding. Let's get started.

8

CREATING EVERYONE@

How to Build a Revolutionary Diversity Initiative at Any Company

Diversity initiatives can be powerful forces for positive change, and they present POC with massive opportunities to be visible and take leadership roles. But their positive impacts are limited to the companies they serve, not extending to the wider world of work. I believe we can change that—and we can do it with Everyone@.

In this chapter, we're going to talk about how to build a diversity program that can be implemented at every company across the United States. Everyone@ is a comprehensive approach to driving diversity, improving productivity, and growing companies' bottom lines. And unlike a standalone diversity initiative, you can take it with you from company to company and use its impact to demonstrate measurable return on investment (ROI)—as well as your leadership skills.

Imagine leading Everyone@Google. Or Everyone@Pinterest. Or Everyone@[your current company]. Fortunately, you don't have to imagine. We're going to show exactly how you can lead the change we need and bring truly everyone—not just POC—to the table.

Building Your Business Case

No diversity-and-inclusion initiative will get off the ground without executive and employee buy-in. You may know it's the right solution for your organization, but without data and research to back you up, you're asking for money based on a hunch. To that end, the surest way to get your colleagues and superiors to take D&I seriously is by proving the business case for it. But before doing so, you have to get the right approvals and involve your HR team.

In the process of putting your case together, you'll also lay out a charter and execution plan that will make actually establishing Everyone@ in your company much easier. It's time to get really familiar with spreadsheets.

We reviewed some of the key research findings that demonstrate the need for diverse businesses in chapter 1. Now you'll use that information to create a coherent and persuasive plan. You'll leverage that plan to not only get buy-in from organizational leadership, but also as a road map for building Everyone@.

Let me stress that this isn't a morality play. This is not—I repeat, not—a feel-good mission. Feel-good is great, but there's a limit to human passion; once it's exhausted, organization and planning, not warm fuzzies, will deliver results. In business, the path to hearts and minds begins with the bottom line, so it's time to show how a more diverse workforce delivers ROI.

The essential parts of your business plan should be:

- An introduction and mission statement that summarizes the problem, the proposed solution, and the forecasted benefits of that solution

- A needs assessment that demonstrates the specific gaps in your organization's culture
- A proposed solution and explanation of benefits
- Specifics about how you'll execute your solution
- Metrics for measuring success

We'll review each of those essentials shortly, but first, let's talk about allies. Before you go to the trouble of creating a full business plan or approaching anyone at the executive level, it's critical that you have your manager's political and administrative backing. First of all, it's simply a best practice to tell your manager about any extracurricular activities related to the workplace. Second, and more important, your manager is a valuable ally—they're your testing ground for ideas and can help broker discussions with other departments or divisions, socialize your initiatives with executives, and carve out realistic timetables and budgets for your program. Involve them early and update them often. Make this part of your weekly and monthly one-on-ones.

Your mentor is another ally to bring in early on. Every time you complete one of these steps, run your deliverable by your mentor as a gut check. Ask them for honest feedback; they should be poking holes in your argument now, so that when you get in front of your executives, your talking points are airtight.

INTRODUCTION AND MISSION STATEMENT

Begin your business case with a short summary of the problem as you see it, based on the reporting you conduct in your needs assessment (more on this shortly). Briefly outline where the gaps exist in current diversity policy and programming. Keep it concise and objective. This is not an emotional exorcism, nor is it a place to rail against the unfairness of the world at large.

Instead, focus most of the introduction on your mission statement. What goal will Everyone@ strive to fulfill, and what other potential benefits will your organization reap as a result? We've already covered some of those benefits in earlier chapters, but you should identify the ones that speak to the most pressing concerns of upper management and lead with them. For example, if revenue is a hot-button issue this year (and when is it not?), you might use the McKinsey study that found a direct correlation between racial and ethnic diversity and financial performance.[69] Then there are cost savings, public relations, and liability issues. You may wish to point out that in 2017 alone, the Equal Employment Opportunity Commission secured nearly half a billion dollars for victims of workplace discrimination.[70] A strong diversity initiative like Everyone@ can mitigate losses from lawsuits.

If you think broad statistics like these won't appeal to your audience, focus on softer benefits specific to your organization. Think employee satisfaction, promotion rates, and retention. Just make sure you've documented the baseline numbers here, so you can report on progress against those metrics later. The more closely you can tailor the benefits of Everyone@ to your organization's objectives, whatever those objectives are, the more likely you'll be to earn their support.

NEEDS ASSESSMENT

You can't prove that your organization will benefit from Everyone@ if you can't demonstrate what it's missing out on without it. A needs assessment identifies the gaps in your organizational culture through detailed reporting and interviews with colleagues, sets the stage for your proposed solution, and provides a useful yardstick for measuring success later.

It helps to establish categories within your needs assessment before you conduct reporting. If you can organize the results of your research by trait, the solutions become much easier to sell to stakeholders. For example, you might assess gaps as well as the presence and quality of these three elements:

Published, enforceable policies on diversity and inclusion at the corporate level. I refer to organized, management-sanctioned opportunities, formal or informal, for discussion and debate of topics related to diversity and inclusion, or of topics that are particularly important to POC. Let's call these "forums."

Opportunities for active engagement. These include lectures, workshops, drives, games, fun runs, or any other company-organized activities that directly promote diversity within your organization. We'll call these "events."

The ability to avoid embarrassing and costly public relations disasters. Enable marketing, sales, public relations, or product development groups to run concepts and product messaging by a diverse team, prior to release, to avoid offending or alienating some communities. Let's call this "community validation."

I suggest a multipronged approach to conducting a needs assessment. Be transparent about your intentions; ultimately, you're seeking solutions that will benefit the entire organization. Seek out suggestions for solutions even as you document the gaps. Utilize any or all of the following methods to gather information:

Published employee handbooks, event calendars, and human resources memos. The first step is to gather everything your organization is already doing in the area of diversity and inclusion. Human resources can be a huge help in gathering these materials for you, especially if your organization spans multiple locations. Summarize your findings on a whiteboard and look for saturation in one area—for example, does your company have a robust policy around diversity but few, if any, related activities? This highlights a need for resources, organization, and accountability on the part of management, human resources, and fellow colleagues.

Interviews with colleagues. Working with your HR department and with an HR professional in the room, invite five to seven colleagues to talk privately about any interaction or engagement they've had with existing D&I initiatives at your company. How did it compare to other places they've worked? Do they feel comfortable bringing up their backgrounds in conversations with colleagues, or do they feel pressure to blend in with the majority culture? Have they sought sponsorship for diversity-related activities? What was the response?

Be sure to interview a range of individuals—POC, certainly, but also women, LGBTQ, and others from diverse backgrounds, as well as majority colleagues. As we've seen in previous chapters, everyone has a stake in creating a more inclusive workplace. The more open you are to all points of view, the stronger your case will be. Resist the urge to get defensive or point fingers. Your HR team should make it clear these conversations will be confidential and that any feedback they give will be anonymized in your reporting. This is not about gathering damaging intel. It's about creating opportunities for positive change.

To that end, your needs assessment can also function as a solutions-gathering exercise. Chances are you're not the only one with ideas for how to improve company culture. Ask your interviewees about the specific changes they'd like to see in policies, forums, or events, and for permission to share the best in your proposal, with appropriate attribution.

Census and demographic data. Some diversity-focused programs suggest pulling local demographic data to demonstrate disparities in the minority- or majority-employee population compared to the overall population of the city, state, or country.[71] Depending on whether you're located in an urban or rural area, how many of your colleagues are commuters, and the availability of local talent for your particular line of work, this may or may not be valuable. You'll need to use your judgment here.

Initiatives conducted by similar nonprofits or organizations. There are a host of organizations doing impressive work in the area of diversity and inclusion. Some are in-house human resources departments; you'll often find documentation of their work on the company's blog or Careers page. Others are nonprofits dedicated to helping businesses diversify. They're constantly publishing stats, best practices, case studies, and presentations on their own sites or in trade publications. Look for write-ups on businesses with a head count similar to yours. How does their breakdown of published policy, forums, and activities compare to yours? How does your organization fare against the best practices published by these nonprofits?

PROPOSED SOLUTION

Now that you've identified the gaps in your company's diversity-and-inclusion efforts, it's time to sell the solution. Go back to the drawing board and the traits you developed as part of the needs assessment: forums, events, and community validation. Now answer the following questions:

- How does Everyone@ address the gaps you found in each of these areas?
- How will you measure its success?
- Why are you the best person to lead it?

Don't worry about including each and every event, seminar, or forum you plan to hold. Instead, speak to Everyone@ as a whole—its mission and goals, the core values it will promote, the people it will serve, and the methods you'll use to reach those people. Provide a basic overview of potential programming, and explain how it will fulfill the needs you've identified. Finally, reiterate the benefits—financial, reputational, operational, or otherwise—your company will see from the successful implementation of this initiative.

PLAN FOR EXECUTION

In identifying needs and proposing solutions, you've answered the "why" behind your Everyone@. Now it's time to answer the "how." No executive, no matter how committed they are to improving diversity and inclusion, will greenlight your initiative without understanding how you plan to actually carry it out. From budget to oversight to communications, it's critical that you address as much as you can in this business case. Such forethought will lend you credibility and make it easier to argue for resources.

Here are some key questions you'll need to answer immediately. Some answers you'll glean from the research you've done into other organizations; others can be answered by your human resources department.

GOVERNANCE

- Which executive(s) will sponsor Everyone@, and what level of involvement will they have?
- How will members be selected, and who's eligible to join?
- Will a steering committee be selected and, if so, what's its role?
- What other subcommittees will be needed?
- How many members will be needed for each subcommittee, and what functions will they fulfill?
- How often will you meet?
- How often will subcommittees meet?

- How will Everyone@ partner with existing ERGs?
- Will Everyone@ have the opportunity to review and make suggestions for changes to company diversity policy?
- How much time will members spend on meetings, programming, administration, and communication?
- How much of that activity, if any, will be conducted during business hours?

PROGRAMMING

- How will forums and events be selected?
- How often will programs run?
- Will non-committee members have a say in programming?
- Will outside speakers be brought in?
- What percentage of programming will be conducted off-site?

COMMUNICATIONS

- How will Everyone@ communicate with employees?
- How will Everyone@ communicate with clients or the public?

RISK AND LIABILITY

- Does the company's risk policy cover off-site events?
- Is employee sponsorship or managerial approval required for outside speakers?
- Are employees permitted to officially represent the company at rallies, marches, or other gatherings?
- Are there security concerns associated with rally or march attendance?

LOGISTICS

- Will common areas, conference rooms, or audio/visual or technology equipment needs to be reserved for Everyone@ subcommittee meetings, forums, and events?
- Who will coordinate booking space?
- How will employees get to off-site events?

BUDGET

- What's the estimated spend for activities, including space, speaker fees, AV/IT needs, transportation to and from events, and administration?
- How much is required from the company to run Everyone@ for a year?
- Will Everyone@ or any committee engage in fundraising activities on or off-site to supplement the company budget?

ACCOUNTABILITY

- How will you collect and incorporate feedback from employees?
- How and when will Everyone@ report on performance?

The answers to these questions will—and should—vary from company to company. It's going to be up to you to tailor Everyone@ to your business's needs and goals, and that, I think, is what makes this concept so unique and powerful. It's not a one-size-fits-all approach, but rather it's agile and flexible, capable of serving each company's different needs.

MEASURING SUCCESS

With an execution plan in place, your last task is to establish metrics by which you can measure your success. It may seem a little silly to talk about performance measurements before you've even implemented the program, but trust me, you'll be thankful a year from now when you write a report and ask for more resources.

As with the rest of your business case, your metrics need to be objective, specific, and tied to the needs you identified in your assessment. They also need to be realistic and relatively easy to prove. If you argued that Everyone@ would save the company money and enhance its reputation, you'd better be able to document that at year-end. Anecdotal evidence will not cut it, unless it's supplementing an employee or customer survey.

Fortunately, there are numerous metrics you can use to demonstrate the value of Everyone@. Nonprofit organizations and state and federal bodies often publish their metrics and can be a good starting place for developing your own set. Here are a few to consider, adapted from those published by the State Human Resources division of Washington state's Office of Financial Management.[72]

Representation. A year in, have employee demographics shifted to more closely align with overall population demographics?

Rates of promotion. Are POC being promoted at the same rate and pay scale as majority employees?

Turnover. Have the employees who've left been primarily POC or other minorities? Has turnover decreased, and can this be at all connected to the diversity initiative?

Employee satisfaction. How have attitudes about workplace diversity and inclusion shifted, if at all, in the last year?

Policy updates. Do all employee policies reflect the mission and goals of Everyone@?

Outreach. How often has Everyone@ engaged employees in discussion or education on relevant issues?

No matter how you choose to measure success, be patient. This won't be an overnight success; you'll need to build trust among your colleagues and executives. You'll have to conduct listening exercises, gather feedback, and incorporate new ideas. Don't expect to have significant data for at least a year into your initiative. Once you do, however, get it in front of leadership as well as the company at large. Build a communications campaign on it—blog posts, lightning talks, maybe even a case study. Your corporate communications department can help you evangelize. Your HR counterpart will also be invaluable here.

Best Practices for Running Everyone@

You may have the most solid business case for Everyone@, but it's almost guaranteed that issues and obstacles will crop up, and often. The pressing needs you identified at the beginning may be replaced by others within months. Stay flexible and remember the following:

- Identify and approach your executive sponsor and HR counterpart early.
- Give Everyone@ the greatest possible chance at succeeding by working with someone at the C-level—if not the CEO, then a direct report. They'll bring greater visibility to your efforts and more easily coordinate initiatives across departments and divisions. They'll also have greater access to budget and other resources.
- Ensure that your council is diverse.

This should be a no-brainer, but I'm not just talking about ethnic or gender diversity. Everyone@ should represent all facets of organizational life, and that includes diversity in hierarchy and job function as well. For example, including managers will not only help with idea generation, but also with new employee training and engagement. A human resources representative can help facilitate tough conversations, properly document them, and gut-check potentially risky initiatives. A member who represents the majority can provide useful insight into partnering with key allies.

CREATE AN EVERYONE@ CHARTER

Like your business case, your charter will provide a clear and objective vision for Everyone@. It will lay out Everyone@'s policies and procedures and define roles and responsibilities. It serves as the foundation for your Everyone@ but can be edited and updated as your mission evolves. Writing your founding charter should be one of your first agenda items; it should include:

- Mission statement, including goals and how you plan to fulfill them
- Identification of executive and HR sponsorship
- Criteria for membership and leadership
- Meeting frequency, attendance policy, and standard agenda
- Behavioral expectations for meetings, along with a confidentiality policy
- Anticipated funding sources
- Roles definition and responsibilities
- Subcommittees and task forces
- A charter amendment policy
- Progress measurement plan

COMMIT TO WHAT YOU CAN ACHIEVE

You'll be tempted to try and solve all the problems you've identified at once. Don't. In fact, be conservative in what you bite off; a small, scalable program that builds over time is much more valuable than one that starts big and loses steam halfway through. Set and commit to a few goals for the year. Reserve two or three as stretch goals (nice-to-haves but not essential). Save the rest for years two, three, four, and five.

GET CREATIVE WITH YOUR BUDGET

Chances are you'll start with a small pool of resources, with more available if you prove successful in your initiative. Program accordingly. Not every event needs to be a blockbuster, not every speaker a national icon. Instead, look for new angles in how you address issues of D&I. Maybe it's an online course in cognitive biases or a guided discussion on a topical theme. There are many ways to add value without spending much.

COMMUNICATE OFTEN

The success of your council will partially depend on how ardent an evangelist you and fellow members are. Use newsletters, intranets, and social media to make sure executives and employees—especially those in minority groups—are aware of and engaging in your programming. Frequent communication also helps increase visibility of the need for diversity and inclusion at your organization, particularly among majority employees.

STICK TO AN AGENDA

I've said that Everyone@ is not a feel-good operation. It's serious business, and serious for your business, and should be treated as such. But it's not a feel-bad operation, either. A poorly governed organization can easily devolve into an opportunity to vent, and vent, and vent, and that does no one—certainly not the employees you represent—any good. While concerns should be aired, keep members on track with an agenda, and follow up with meeting minutes to show them what they've accomplished by staying within bounds.

BUILD STRATEGIC PARTNERSHIPS

Some of your best work will be collaborative. Look to other like-minded groups and councils within your organization for ideas, cosponsorship of events, and help with logistics. Pay special attention to your ERGs and consider integrating their leadership into the council as part of a special subcommittee. They can help with communications and rallying troops for your events, while also providing valuable feedback on your various initiatives.

SHARE CREDIT

You may be your organization's diversity champion, but you won't be leading this initiative alone. Prepare for lots of ideas—solicited and unsolicited, good and not so good. Be open and diplomatic but don't be afraid to push back when resources are on the line. And when you receive a winning idea or put on a well-received event, share the accolades with members and sponsors. After all, a truly inclusive workplace celebrates every person's contribution.

There's no single right way to run Everyone@. You'll likely falter a few times as you expand your programming to include more and more employees. That's fine. Learn from your mistakes, document everything, and seek advice early and often.

9

RAISING YOUR HAND

How Entry-Level and Mid-Career Professionals Can Have a Measurable Effect on an Organization's Diversity

We've discussed several moments in your career when the spotlight will inevitably fall on you—moments when you'll be asked to speak for your entire community, even though you shouldn't and can't. There will be moments where your words, actions, and work will be seen as an example of everyone who belongs to your community, even though that's as absurd as it is unfair. And when the topic of building a more diverse workforce comes up—and it will come up—all eyes in the room are going to shift your way yet again.

Although the spotlight may be uncomfortable, it's a moment you should seize. After all, not everyone gets this opportunity, and when the topic of diversifying an organization's talent pipeline arises, you have yet another chance to shine. Having a thoughtful, informed opinion about diversity recruiting will give you the chance to showcase your research and insight to your peers and manager—and it might even get you noticed by the C-suite.

And who better than you to provide guidance to upper management on building a more diverse workforce? After all, as a person of color, you've experienced the challenges of the hiring process that might not be present for the majority. You can use that experience—as well as the research and insights provided in this book—to articulate a strategy that ultimately can help your organization become more diverse.

Management and Mid-Career Professionals

When you look at your company's senior leadership, are members of your community present? If not, you're hardly alone. POC in the C-suite are rare. In fact, among Fortune 500 companies, just three CEOs are Black. And since the 2016 departure of former Xerox CEO Ursula Burns—the first Black woman to run a Fortune 500 company—all of them are men. Diversity among corporate boards is somewhat better, but only just. As of 2016, 22% of new appointees to corporate boards were Black, but Black executives still made up just over 9% of all board membership, and Latinx members accounted for slightly more than 6%.[73]

With this in mind, it's wiser for organizations to focus on attracting entry- to mid-level professionals of color—and ensuring there are internal strategies in place to help them succeed and feel included. But attracting less senior employees isn't simple or easy. And it's not just a matter of casting a wider net or devoting additional resources. While both of those tactics are valid and valuable, they're not enough to have a measurable effect on the overall diversity of the company you work for.

Transferable Skills Are Critical

The key to making the mid-level of a company more representative is focusing on transferable skills. These are abilities and experiences that may have been learned, applied, and honed in another industry or function. For example, a successful outside sales executive for a recruiting firm will have a number of skills and experiences that can transfer to a role selling software-as-a-service (SaaS). This salesperson has advanced knowledge of sales tactics and will have experience tailoring a solution to a business's needs. And because she's experienced at selling a business-to-business talent solution, she can easily apply that knowledge to selling a business-to-business software solution.

And this is especially valuable for newer industries. With so few POC employed in these industries, the organization you work for is unlikely to find the candidate it needs if management looks only for people within your own industry or at a competitor. Instead, they need to expand their search to include people from other industries who have transferable skills. With a little training and education, those workers can adapt their abilities and experiences to your industry with ease. Plus, the company will get valuable new perspectives and best practices from outside the industry, which can help improve a variety of processes.

I know this, because I've lived it. During my second year in finance, I decided I wanted to make a career transition and seek opportunities in the tech industry. I applied to more than twenty jobs, ranging from publicly traded companies to my friend's startup. I always made it to the phone screen but rarely made it to the real interview.

In the rare instances when I did make it past the phone screen, I was regularly told I didn't have "tech industry" experience and therefore wasn't qualified for the role. The most frustrating part of the experience was that many of the job postings I was replying to listed skill sets that I have and have demonstrated throughout my career:

- Detail oriented
- Customer-centric
- Self-starter
- Experience with CRMs
- Previous technical sales experience

The "previous technical sales experience" was the bane of my existence. Not having that specific experience in my background prevented me from breaking into the tech industry, despite the fact that I worked at one of the most prestigious and competitive organizations in the business world. This was the story time after time—until I finally made it to a final round of interviews with one technology company in their Washington, DC, office.

The interviews went well, and after meeting with the entire team, I felt fairly confident I was going to receive an offer. After all, it was an entry-level operations role requiring one to two years of previous work experience. The next day, my heart sank when the hiring manager called me to say they were moving forward with another candidate who had previous experience working at a smaller tech company. This person, they felt, would be better able to adapt to a "startup" setting, given that they were launching their presence in DC.

That's when I decided to build my own tech company. And four years later, the woman who had given me the devastating news about not being qualified for this entry-level role sat in my conference room to discuss opportunities at Jopwell. Funny how the world works sometimes.

Develop a Diversity-Focused Referral Program

Wait a minute—didn't I say earlier in this book that referral programs were sure to be a source of sameness? I did. But such programs that prioritize diversity and incentivize employees to refer diverse candidates can be a tremendously effective way to create a more representative workforce. In fact, consulting giant Accenture has implemented such a program.

In addition to its existing referral bonuses, the company pays employees an additional bonus if a candidate they referred who's Black, Hispanic, female, or a military veteran gets hired.[74] Suggesting a program like this is a terrific way to draw attention to your organization's diversity deficiency and help your colleagues be a part of the solution.

Create an Early-Talent Pipeline

When it comes to creating a more representative workforce, there's no bigger or more effective opportunity than early talent—that is, recent college graduates and university students. These are a company's best bets for diversifying its workforce, and every growing company with fifty or more employees should have a comprehensive strategy in place to attract and promote them.

No, I'm not making a case for age discrimination here. Every age and professional level matters when it comes to creating a more diverse workforce. But early talent presents a special opportunity to capture young professionals who are just beginning to explore the workforce. They have yet to develop preconceived notions while working at other companies, and they're very likely to tell their friends and families about your organization and its diverse and inclusive culture, leading to greater mindshare among and more referrals from diverse communities. And, most important, they're an investment in the future of your business. By diversifying the employee pipeline at the entry point, companies set the stage for a more representative staff in the future.

To capture early talent, a company needs to start, well, early. In this case, that means building and investing in a campus recruiting program. When done well, a recruiting program can be a company's best asset for creating a stable, reliable pipeline of talent—both diverse and otherwise. In fact, a 2015 study by the Human Capital Institute found that businesses that are confident in their talent pipeline recruit twice as many recent graduates as those that have little confidence in their pipeline.[75] The study also found that, for businesses with active campus recruiting efforts, the following were the most effective sources for quality talent:

- Training programs for recent graduates
- Apprenticeships
- Internships and co-ops
- Having employees mentor students

I can personally attest that each of these offerings works—and works well. In fact, it was a campus recruiting program that led me to Goldman Sachs. While I was in college, I secured a summer internship there, and I came back for two more summer internships before being offered a job once I graduated. It made me feel invested in the company, and, perhaps more important, it made me feel as though they were investing in me, too. I knew that a company that was willing to give me three internships, along with the training and growth I received along the way, was one I wanted to launch my career with. It also made me a brand ambassador for the firm on campus. If someone wanted to know about the firm or about my internship experiences there, I was more than happy to tell them.

Of course, it's not just Goldman Sachs that invests in campus recruiting. Every major bank and financial services firm does the same, and for good reason: they know it works.

Build a Campus Recruitment Program

With so much riding on an early-talent pipeline, companies have to get their campus recruiting program right. Here are some key strategies every successful program shares.

BEFORE ANYTHING ELSE, DEFINE QUALITY

Companies have to hire for key skills and abilities, not just for the community they come from. So before a company takes any steps toward building an early-talent pipeline, it must define what it's looking for.

First, it must identify priority entry-level positions. These will likely be roles with multiple open positions, as well as ones that serve key business functions, such as entry-level engineers, IT associates, or inside sales representatives. Once the positions are identified, the next step is specifying the majors these positions require, or at least the majors that top performers have held in the recent past.

Next, the company needs to identify its most significant performance characteristics. This entails setting a baseline for GPA, and considering evaluating students' GPAs in the major, as well as their overall GPA. After all, a student who's particularly strong in their chosen field but weaker in unrelated coursework may still be a great fit for the roles the company needs to fill. Other factors to consider include the candidate's involvement in athletics, student organizations, or volunteer work. These should be secondary to GPA but may also give insight into a student's interests, priorities, ambitions, and leadership abilities.

Once the hirer has taken these steps, they should have a clear definition of the kind of student the company is targeting. They'll know, for example, that they're looking for students majoring in computer science who meet a GPA cutoff and can boast extracurricular activities. With this knowledge, the company can take the next steps: building a plan to find those candidates.

USE THE COMPANY'S BEST, MOST RELATABLE PEOPLE

When attempting to get diverse students interested in an organization, the company needs to take advantage of existing employees with whom diverse candidates are most likely to relate. Companies shouldn't just send whoever might be available in human resources or recruiting to a college campus. The ideal recruiters are relatable, enthusiastic, and passionate about the company's brand. In a perfect world, they would be relatively young professionals who entered the company through an internship or existing campus recruiting program. The right people may not even be in recruiting. If their managers can spare them, they may be interested in participating in the program as an off-site activity.

PREPARE THE NARRATIVE

Today's early talent is more informed than ever before about which companies they want to work for and the missions and values of those companies. Much has been written about Millennials' and Gen Z's interest in companies' commitment to issues like social good, environmental impact, and corporate responsibility, and if you're a young person of color, you probably know what you value in a potential employer. This is why so many major corporations are now showcasing their mission statements, their commitments to diversity and inclusion, and all the ways they give back to the community. Those are all great things, and I support them 100%. But there are some key things companies still overlook when it comes to recruiting early talent: company culture and potential for growth.

In fact, a study by Collegefeed.com (now AfterCollege.com) polled sixty thousand millennial students and recent grads about which companies they most want to work for, what they look for in an employer, and how they heard about those companies. One of the most shocking findings from that survey is that the top two attributes they look for in an employer are "people and culture fit" and "growth potential."[76]

With this in mind, everyone representing a company to early talent needs talking points and leave-behind materials about these very items. This could be a one-sheeter covering "a day in the life" of a recent grad working at the company. Ambassadors must be up-to-date on professional development initiatives and capable of speaking to an organization's commitment to individual growth and continuous learning. And they must remember to give students their contact information so they can stay in touch throughout the rest of the year!

Don't get me wrong—a company's values and mission matter, and representatives should showcase those in their campus recruiting materials. But they shouldn't prioritize them over the other factors that matter to students and recent grads. Balance is key.

MEET THEM WHERE THEY ARE

Since it's commonly called "campus recruiting," it's easy to see why so many employers make the mistake of thinking that recruiting early talent happens mainly—or only—on university campuses. Sure, that's a large and critical component, but when building a truly effective early-talent pipeline, it's only one component out of many. Career fairs and recruiting events are great ways to be visible and get the workforce of tomorrow interested in and engaged with an organization, but in today's always-connected world, it's not the only way to reach early talent.

PUT IT ALL TOGETHER: YOUR ELEVATOR PITCH FOR DIVERSITY

When it comes to building an early-talent pipeline, you need a mission statement that tells future young professionals about what your brand is and what it values in a succinct sentence. For today's college students, that means crafting a statement that ties your business goals back to how you're serving the community, the environment, or even both! Here are a few mission statements that do just that.

Patagonia: Build the best product, cause no unnecessary harm, use business to inspire and implement solutions to the environmental crisis.

Warby Parker: To offer designer eyewear at a revolutionary price, while leading the way for socially conscious businesses.

What do these statements have in common? They're aligning commerce with social good and positive impact. In just a sentence, they're conveying their brands' values and showcasing the fact that they intend to use business success to build a better world. With this in mind, you will be prepared to help your company develop the sentence that reflects how diverse students will perceive your workplace.

Millennials are always online, and this means every company's early-talent presence should be as well. If the company has the resources, it should consider creating social media accounts dedicated to early-talent recruiting and engaging with students and recent grads and sharing relevant news and thought leadership content that they'll be interested in. Twitter is great for connecting in real time and answering questions early talent may have about the organization. LinkedIn is another great channel for sharing content and showcasing news and development. Many large organizations also maintain student-focused recruiting pages on their primary website that inform readers about company culture, values, and what it's like to work there. A monthly email newsletter that early talent can subscribe to is another terrific forum for engaging and sharing news. In short, companies must think beyond the physical campus and expand early-talent recruiting efforts to where today's students live online.

This isn't a fad. Millennials turn to social media for a variety of things, and Generation Z, who will be entering the workforce soon enough, is just as connected—even more so.

DEVELOP KEY INFLUENCERS—AND KEEP THEM ENGAGED THROUGHOUT THE YEAR

The Collegefeed.com study referenced earlier also found hard proof for something most of us already know: the number-one way we find out about companies is through our friends.[77] Our friends tend to share our interests, values, and—typically—our ambitions, so we trust what our friends have to say about potential employers. This is why cultivating brand ambassadors on campus is critical for building an early-talent pipeline.

Consider what we've learned in recent years from the rise of a practice known as "influencer marketing"—leveraging people with active and engaged followers on social media to create brand awareness or increase brand affinity. If you've ever watched an unboxing video on YouTube or seen an Instagram celebrity rave about a product they love, it's likely that a marketer at the company whose products they're gushing about incentivized them to do so. It's simple, but it's incredibly effective, especially among younger consumers. In fact, 94% of marketers find it effective, and it can generate eleven times the ROI of traditional advertising.[78] Those are powerful numbers, and the company you work for can generate similar results with its talent pipeline—if done in the right way.

First off, the outreach messaging has to be authentic. Millennials and Generation Z are inundated with more content—and thus, more ads—than any generation before them. We've seen so much content from brands trying to capture the zeitgeist or capitalize on trends in ham-handed, tone-deaf ways. When we spot it—and we can spot it a mile away—it's an immediate turnoff. For campus ambassadors to be effective, they have to genuinely reflect the company's mission, values, and culture. That means they must be brought in, treated like valued and trusted assets, and made team members from the beginning.

Let's say the company has a large crop of summer interns. Toward the end of the summer, the company should identify the ones who will return to school in the fall and look to identify those whose work and level of engagement stood out to their managers. These will become potential campus ambassadors.

Once identified, they can be asked if they'd be willing to continue to engage with the company throughout the year as official campus ambassadors. They should be onboard for regular communication between the company and the ambassadors, attending events and sharing information and materials about the company around campus. They should even host informal public informational sessions for other students a few times throughout the school year. In a perfect world, the company can offer them a stipend of a few thousand dollars per semester. This shows a serious commitment to them as soon-to-be young professionals as well as appreciation and understanding of the work they're being asked to do on the company's behalf.

The ambassadors will also need a designated person at the company to be their primary point of contact. That person should be willing and able to check in with the ambassadors monthly and provide answers to questions and updates on important changes and developments at the company.

THINK PROGRAMMATICALLY

Imagine starting a new role with ten other young professionals, each of whom will be doing the same job. Now imagine you're the only person of color in the group. No matter how welcoming your peers and manager are or how inclusive the environment, you're likely going to feel at least somewhat like an outsider. This will almost certainly lead to an eventual loss of engagement, burnout, and possibly even poor performance. As I've addressed several times over the course of this book, no matter how hard you work, if you don't feel as though you can be your true self, you're going to have a hard time giving 100% and making the biggest impact possible.

That's the kind of thinking that initially drove the founders of the Posse Foundation. They realized that talented students from diverse backgrounds were getting into colleges but failing to thrive for these very reasons. On paper, these students should have prospered in academia, but the data showed that they weren't—and on a massive scale. So for nearly thirty years, they've been helping talented students from diverse backgrounds enter the university in cohorts of ten students, each with diverse backgrounds. The results have been nothing short of astounding: Posse Scholars, as they call their students, have a graduation rate of 90%, and 80% of the class of 2017 served as officers of a college organization. Some 20% of those served as student body president. These statistics are all the more impressive once you realize that 57% are first-generation college students.[79]

With this in mind, imagine that, of those same ten people you entered the workforce with, at least half were POC. Would you feel more comfortable in your own skin? Would you find it easier to relate and share your best self at work? Of course you would. That's a win for you, and it's a win for your employer, since they'll be able to realize your full potential and the difference you can truly make.

This is why programmatic hiring initiatives are perfect for diversifying a company's workforce. When a company can hire in cohorts, it can radically reshape the experience that diverse professionals have within the organization.

This is also why I launched a programmatic hiring initiative at Jopwell. There are qualified entry- and mid-level candidates from all industries with transferable skills who have worked at competitive organizations and found ways to succeed. There's no reason to believe they wouldn't succeed in the organizations that partner with Jopwell if given a chance.

That's why we're encouraging companies that partner with Jopwell to treat our cohort of candidates as they would any other internally referred candidate and give them the benefit of the doubt if they have transferable skills. Through this initiative, companies:

- Connect with Jopwell's mid-level professionals through multiple channels, including our platform and curated exclusive events.
- Engage with Jopwell community members through Jopwell Talks, our large-scale community event series.
- Hire top professionals with the direct or transferable skills they need to make an impact on Day One.

The initiatives happen in a three-step process:

Companies choose one or multiple cohorts, including candidates in a variety of fields. After a company makes their selection, we'll build five distinct classes, consisting of ten prescreened candidates who will engage with the customer over the course of twelve months.

We then assist companies with curating social events to engage each class of Jopwell users. Social events range from dinners to sporting events to in-office visits. The point of the event is to humanize the hiring process and authentically connect with our users.

Through Jopwell Talks (our community event series), companies have the opportunity to be a sponsor of the event series with the theme of "being a person of color in corporate America." Jopwell Talks bring together Jopwell's community, partners, diversity experts, and influencers to engage in authentic conversations. Companies that participate are encouraged to bring their employees to demonstrate their investment in diversity initiatives.

The next time the company you work for plans to hire multiple people, encourage the decision-makers to make a concerted effort to make each cohort diverse. Remind them that diverse teams perform better and that the company will experience gains in engagement and retention as well. This strategy doesn't require massive changes to implement. It just requires a thoughtful approach to hiring and onboarding that makes diversity a priority. It's that simple.

General Best Practices

When it comes to diversity, there are some established best practices and accepted wisdom that apply to every role, no matter the professional level, field, or function. Much has been written about these practices, but as a person of color, you can lend your insights when communicating them to leadership, and you have instant credibility when discussing them—something a writer on a human resources blog, for example, may lack. These advantages can help you drive these practices with your peers and company leadership, so don't shy away from bringing them up when applicable and appropriate.

BE READY TO HAVE THE "QUALITY" DISCUSSION

When implementing diversity strategies, you'll inevitably hear that any programmatic approach to diversity hiring will lower the bar for the quality of candidates coming into the organization. In these instances, it's imperative to clearly articulate the value of diversity in the workforce.

You'll need to stand firm and confidently present the truth: that diversity programs actually ensure that the best workforce is being hired, as the company will be incorporating differing thoughts, opinions, backgrounds, and experiences into the workforce. Doing so will push the company to be more innovative and disruptive, rather than maintaining the status quo.

SHOW DON'T TELL

No matter how seriously an organization views the issue of diversity and inclusion, if its public persona doesn't reflect that, it's going to struggle to find and retain diverse talent. This is yet another opportunity to help your employer diversify its workforce. Look at your company's website and marketing materials. Are POC present and reflected? What about on the Careers page? If not, how seriously do you think diverse candidates will take the company's messaging about its commitment to diversity? And if POC are visible in the marketing materials, are they actual employees or just stock images? Stock imagery, even when selected and edited carefully, is usually obviously unreal, and if a company is trying to convince its audience that its workforce is diverse but doesn't have employees of color to showcase on its site, no one's going to take it seriously. If there's a way to graciously share these insights with your marketing team, do so—and offer to help them showcase diversity more effectively.

Another place where images come into play is thought leadership. Think about who represents your company's brand online via blog posts, press releases, podcasts, conferences, and the like. Are diverse voices present there? If not, consider remedying that. Most companies have a handful of people they send out to give talks and interviews with media outlets, and they can gain a great deal of mindshare with diverse communities by adding POC to that rotation.

RETHINK YOUR JOB POSTINGS

Think back to what I mentioned earlier about mid-career professionals and transferable skills. When you look at your company's job postings online, do you find requirements that might discourage people who have transferable skills that could succeed in the organization? For example, if a company is looking for five to seven years of industry-specific sales experience, it might lose its shot at landing a talented salesperson looking to change industries, one whose skills might be exactly the shot in the arm the sales team needs. So limit the requirements to must-haves and allow those with transferable skills to see that they have a shot, too.

Companies should also make sure to call out their commitment to diversity and inclusion in job postings. It's a small thing, but it can go a long way toward signaling to the talent pool that they won't be discriminated against in the hiring process. This language can live at the end of a job posting and on the overall Careers page. Viacom's language is a great example, and—even better—the following text lives at the top of the Careers page on their website.

> *At Viacom, the spirit of inclusion feeds into everything that we do, on-screen and off. From the programming and movies we create to employee benefits/programs and Viacommunity outreach initiatives, we believe that opportunity, access, resources and rewards should be available to and for the benefit of all. Viacom is proud to be an equal opportunity workplace and is an affirmative action employer. We are committed to equal employment opportunity regardless of race, color, ethnicity, ancestry, religion, creed, sex, national origin, sexual orientation, age, citizenship status, marital status, disability, gender identity, gender expression, and Veteran status.*
>
> *At Viacom, we have a clear vision: to be the place where a diverse mix of talented people want to come, to stay and do their best work. We pride ourselves on bringing the best entertainment to our audiences around the world, and we know our company runs on the hard work and dedication of our passionate and creative employees.*
>
> *Viacom's dedication to promoting diversity, multiculturalism, and inclusion is clearly reflected in all of our content and across all of our brands. Diversity is more than a commitment at Viacom—it is the foundation of what we do. We are fully focused on equality and believe deeply in diversity of race, gender, sexual orientation, religion, ethnicity, national origin, and all the other fascinating characteristics that make us different.*[80]

This language signals two things to diverse professionals: Viacom is aware of the value of diversity, and they've made it such a priority that this messaging dominates the first half of their Careers page. In fact, aside from links, there's no other copy on the page. This is far better than, say, having a stand-alone diversity page that pays lip service to hiring POC. Anyone can add a page like that—but when a company of Viacom's size and influence doubles down on diversity in this fashion, you tend to take it seriously.

Be Informed

Even if you don't have the opportunity to directly contribute to your company's diversity initiatives, you can at least have an informed opinion on the subject, based on statistics and the established best practices I've just outlined. Referencing this information and these ideas will dazzle your peers and managers and help your organization move in a positive direction toward diversity and inclusion. It'll be a win for your career, a win for your company, and a win for diverse professionals everywhere.

10

MOVING FORWARD

Stepping Up and Strapping In for the Ride Ahead

Thank you so much for coming on this journey with me. In writing this book, I've done a ton of research and talked to countless people who have taught me more than I ever thought possible. It's been an incredible ride, and the stories I've heard and the things I've learned have been as humbling as they've been awe-inspiring. But we're not quite done yet.

Over the course of this book, we've talked about everything from the history of workplace diversity to becoming the best possible employee—and your best possible self. I've asked a lot of you as well. I've challenged you to speak up, step outside of your comfort zone, and take the lead on making the American workforce more representative of the country's many cultures and ethnicities. None of those things are easy, and I'm well aware of just how much I'm asking of you. It's no less than I've asked of myself over the past few years as cofounder and CEO of Jopwell. But I can't end this journey without asking you to do a few more things.

First of all, be patient.

The change we represent is coming. It has to. Every year, more and more businesses come around to what some Silicon Valley companies have been trying to accomplish for years. Those companies realize the true value of a diverse workforce and the effect it can have on their bottom lines. And as demographics in the United States continue to change, employers will have no choice but to target historically underrepresented communities to find the talent they need to stay competitive. We can lead this change, and we can lend our voices and perspectives to our employers to accelerate the change in our own workplaces. But it's not going to happen overnight.

As we saw in chapter 1, positive progress is rarely immediate or linear. For every two steps forward, expect to take one step back. We're playing the long game here, and expecting overnight progress will only lead to exhaustion, frustration, and fatigue. You can't allow yourself to become burned out, and we can't afford to lose you. It's going to be difficult, but it can be done. I can think of no better paragon of patience and resilience in the face of opposition than legendary civil rights activist and Nobel Peace Prize winner Nelson Mandela, and there's much we can learn from his example.

Stay the Course

Mr. Mandela began his outspoken opposition of apartheid—South Africa's former system of institutional discrimination against POC—when he was only in college. Attending a student protest resulted in his expulsion from University College of Fort Hare. After that, he worked a series of jobs in Johannesburg before finally completing his degree at another university. In 1952, he was arrested after leading a campaign of civil disobedience in protest of a number of unjust laws. In 1953, he was banned from attending meetings of any kind or speaking to more than one person at a time for six months. He received similar bans in 1955 and again in 1956.

In 1956, he was arrested and tried for treason. The trial continued until 1961, when all defendants were found not guilty. But the South African establishment was far from finished in its attempt to silence Mr. Mandela.

In 1962, he was arrested yet again—this time for leaving the country without a permit and inciting workers to strike. This charge earned him five years in prison. And the very next year, Mr. Mandela and ten others were charged with sabotage. He was found guilty and sentenced to life in prison. He spent the next twenty-seven years in prison, much of it in a tiny concrete cell, sleeping on a straw mat.

But he never lost his fire. He never gave up on his belief in a unified, nondiscriminatory South Africa. He wrote hundreds of letters and read countless books to better himself and build alliances. Even while imprisoned, he continued to be a force for change. And when he was finally released in 1990, he threw himself back into the fray. Three years later, he was awarded the Nobel Peace Prize. In 1994, he was elected president of South Africa—the first election in which he'd ever voted in his life.[81]

It took over fifty years from the time he began his career in politics for his vision of a unified South Africa to take shape. He suffered censorship, imprisonment, violence, and overwhelming discrimination, but his persistence eventually paid off. Obviously, the change we're looking for is nowhere near as massive, nor does it face nearly as much opposition. But like Mr. Mandela, we have to acknowledge that change happens gradually and strap ourselves in for the long haul. Otherwise, we risk getting burned out and wanting to give up. That leads me to the next thing I'd like you to do: give yourself permission to fail.

In the startup world, we like to say "fail fast, fail often." That means we give ourselves permission to make mistakes, acknowledge that failure is inevitable and not necessarily a bad thing, and prioritize learning from our missteps. It also means we don't dwell on our failures and judge ourselves and our colleagues when failure happens. It's not just a catchphrase. It's a way of approaching business and life.

Every event or program you hold through Everyone@ won't be a resounding success. Not every executive you talk to about the business case for diversity will be receptive. The important thing is to accept that failure is a part of life and work, and you risk failure every time you try something new—but risk is the only path to success.

So don't beat yourself up when something goes wrong. Instead, acknowledge that you failed and look for what you can learn from it. Hold yourself accountable for your mistakes but don't dwell on them or judge yourself harshly. Do your best work, and accept that, while some degree of failure is unavoidable, it's also the price of innovation and success.

After all, as hockey great Wayne Gretzky famously said, "You miss 100% of the shots you don't take."

Avoid Division at All Costs

When we talk about workplace diversity, it can be easy to engage in "us versus them" thinking. But whether it happens instantly or gradually, that mode of thinking will eventually impact how you see yourself and how you behave toward others. Not only will that limit your ability to be your best self at work, but it will also limit your ability to be the change you want to see in the workplace—and in the world.

Humans are tribal creatures at heart. We instinctively sort ourselves into what psychologists call "in-groups" and "out-groups." In-groups are made up of people with whom we share some common bond, whether real or perceived. Out-groups, however, consist of people with whom we have little or no perceived commonalities. If you're a Knicks fan, say, and you see someone on the street wearing a Knicks cap, you're likely to associate yourself with that person and have positive affinity for them, even though the only thing you know about them is the fact that they might be a Knicks fan. If you see someone wearing a Celtics hat, however, you're likely to have the opposite reaction, and you're likely to have it both automatically and subconsciously.

We do this constantly, and we do it with everything from gender to ethnicity to our workplace roles. It's not clear necessarily why humans do this, but boy do we do it a lot. Some scientists theorize that oxytocin—a chemical in our brain known to encourage social behavior—may play a role. In a 2012 study, scientists from the Donders Institute for Brain, Cognition, and Behaviour at Radboud University in the Netherlands, gave one group of men a dose of oxytocin and another group a placebo. Both groups were tasked with rating the attractiveness of unfamiliar symbols. What followed is as fascinating as it is concerning:

> *Before making their decisions, the participants could see the ratings of the other people inside and outside of their group. When the in-group and out-group members' ratings differed, participants given oxytocin conformed more closely to the in-group's scores. This conformity effect was not seen in the placebo group. Together, these findings suggest that oxytocin can influence subjective preferences and may stimulate individuals to conform to the behavior and beliefs of others in their group.*[82]

Though far from conclusive, this study does indicate that our urge to separate ourselves into in-groups and out-groups is to at least some degree biological. That means it's a difficult urge to overcome—but we must resist it at all costs.

We've talked about this before, but it bears repeating: POC alone can't effect the kind of change we're striving for. No single group can. Building more diverse and inclusive workplaces is going to take involvement from everyone, so we as POC can't allow ourselves to see this as "our" issue alone. It's not. It's everyone's issue, and getting everyone involved means resisting the urge to engage in in-group versus out-group behavior.

Nelson Mandela, for example, knew that Black people alone couldn't end apartheid in South Africa. In fact, when a splinter group broke away from the African National Congress to start a congress that would exclude white South Africans, he chided the group as being "immature" and "naïve."[83] Both those terms apply to the notion that any single group can effect massive, sweeping change. To make this happen, we need everyone at the table.

So don't let others create divisions. Don't let yourself create divisions, either. Be mindful of your own thoughts and actions, and stop yourself from judging others impulsively. When you see divisions forming, call them out tactfully and professionally, and attempt to start a dialogue. Be a watchdog for inclusion and remember that true inclusion includes everyone. We need every ally we can get, so don't discount the input from others, no matter who they are. Gather everyone you possibly can to the cause.

Be a Mentor

We've talked a lot in this book about the value of having a mentor. A mentor can provide experienced guidance, wisdom, and access to your company's leadership. They can be a sounding board for ideas and plans for the future. They can help you level up faster than you ever could alone.

And you can do the same for someone else.

Finally, I'd like to challenge you to take what you've learned from your own experiences and what you've learned while reading *Let Them See You*, and use it to mentor a person of color who's younger than you. It doesn't matter if you're twenty-five or fifty-five. Your knowledge and experience are valuable, and they can help someone who's coming up become wiser and more successful.

But don't wait for them to come to you. If a younger colleague has recently joined your company or a professional group to which you belong, introduce yourself and ask if they'd like to get lunch or a coffee. You don't have to say, "I'd like to mentor you." In fact, doing so might come off as a little presumptuous or downright creepy. All you need to do is make a genuine connection and let them know that you're interested and invested in their success. We rarely do that sort of thing for each other, and I think that's a shame.

The old aphorism "A rising tide lifts all boats" applies here. By helping younger POC succeed and navigate the world of work, you're paving the way for future generations to succeed as well. We've traditionally had to work twice as hard as our colleagues to gain recognition and advancement, but as more and more POC enter the workforce, mentoring our younger colleagues can establish a precedent of success and begin to undo decades of misguided and inaccurate misconceptions about our abilities and our commitment to making our employers successful. Most important, it will empower the younger members of our communities to succeed and pay it forward.

EPILOGUE:
Keep Making the Workplace Better

I didn't get here alone. I've benefited from the experience and insight of colleagues, managers, mentors, family members, and friends. They've made me who I am. Though I'm still relatively young, I feel as though I've lived several lifetimes through the wisdom I've gleaned from those around me. That's why I'd like you to share *your* story with me.

Hearing from members of diverse communities helps me gain a better understanding of the passions, priorities, and pain points we experience in the workplace every day. It makes me better at my job, and it makes the incredible team at Jopwell better at helping organizations become more diverse and inclusive. The people who have shared their stories on Jopwell's "The Well" are particularly brave and insightful, and I invite you to step into the spotlight and join them.

Tell me your story. Tell me how you got to where you are. Tell me what you've struggled with along the way. Tell me your hopes and your passions, your fears and your failures. Allow me to learn from your experiences, and help me and the Jopwell team create new paths and opportunities for POC in companies around the country.

Show me—and the world—who you are.

Don't be afraid to be who you truly are at work, no matter how daunting that may seem.

Let them see you.

Be proud of yourself and your community and keep doing great work.

Don't compromise your values, and don't shy away from taking the big risks.

This is our time, friends, and it's up to us to seize the moment and take the lead. Let them know we're here, we're capable, we're united—and we're the future.

APPENDIX:
An Appeal to Business Leaders

Now I'd like to take a moment to address business leaders directly, because you, too, can be a powerful force for change and a vital ally for diverse professionals. Investing in a more diverse workforce within your company isn't just the right thing to do—it's smart business. In a few short years, your customers or end users are going to look very different than how they look today. That's because U.S. demographics are changing rapidly. Meanwhile, the growth rate for the country's "combined minority" groups between today and 2060 is projected to be 74%.[84] By 2030, POC are projected to make up the majority of the population aged thirty-five and under—a prime demographic for a variety of goods and services.[85]

And it's not just population numbers that are changing. Blacks, Asians, and Native Americans had a combined buying power of $2.4 trillion in 2017—156% higher than it was in 2000. Latinx and Hispanic people accounted for $1.5 trillion in buying power.[86] For business-to-consumer businesses, this represents a massive opportunity for growth—and massive potential for failure at a hefty cost, if your marketing and messaging are tone-deaf.

NOTES

1. "Labor Force Characteristics by Race and Ethnicity, 2015," September 2016. bls.gov/opub/reports/race-and-ethnicity/2015/home.htm.
2. "Certificates and Degrees Conferred by Race/Ethnicity," 2017. nces.ed.gov/programs/coe/pdf/coe_svc.pdf.
3. "What percentage of S&E degrees do women and racial/ethnic minorities earn?" 2012. nsf.gov/nsb/sei/edTool/data/college-11.html.
4. "2017 Recruiter Sentiment Survey," 2017. mrinetwork.com/media/304094/2017hiringsentimentstudy.pdf.
5. Siofra Pratt, "The Incredible True Value of an Employee Referral," June 3, 2015. socialtalent.com/blog/the-incredible-true-value-of-an-employee-referral-infographic.
6. Jonathan Sherry, "Data Driving Important Discussions," June 3, 2015. slideshare.net/slideshow/embed_code/key/gL299OELEtADdQ.
7. Lindsay Dunsmuir, "Many Americans Have No Friends of Another Race: Poll," August 8, 2013. reuters.com/article/us-usa-poll-race-idUSBRE97704320130808.

8. Vivian Hunt, Dennis Layton, and Sara Prince, "Why Diversity Matters," January 2015. mckinsey.com/business-functions/organization/our-insights/why-diversity-matters.

9. Megan Rose Dickey, "Snap Says 'Diversity Is About More Than Numbers,'" February 2, 2017. techcrunch.com/2017/02/02/snap-diversity.

10. Jefferson Graham, "Snapchat Under Fire for Marley Filter Called Blackface," April 20, 2016. usatoday.com/story/tech/2016/04/20/snapchat-under-fire-blackface-filter/83284206.

11. Daniel Victor, "Pepsi Pulls Ad Accused of Trivializing Black Lives Matter," April 5, 2017 nytimes.com/2017/04/05/business/kendall-jenner-pepsi-ad.html.

12. Evan Sharp, "Our Plan for a More Diverse Pinterest," July 30, 2015. newsroom.pinterest.com/en/post/our-plan-for-a-more-diverse-pinterest.

13. Ben Silbermann, "A 2016 Update on Diversity at Pinterest," December 15, 2016. blog.pinterest.com/en/post/a-2016-update-on-diversity-at-pinterest.

14. Gunnar Myrdal, *An American Dilemma: The Negro Problem and Modern Democracy*, vol: 2. (New York: Harper & Bros, 1944).

15. William A. Sundstrom, "Last Hired, First Fired? Unemployment and Urban Black Workers During the Great Depression," *Journal of Economic History*, 52, no. 2 (June, 1992): 417

16. Terry H.Anderson, *The Pursuit of Fairness: A History of Affirmative Action* (Oxford: Oxford University Press, 2005), p. 12.

17. Anderson, *The Pursuit of Fairness: A History of Affirmative Action.*

18. "Executive Order 8802," June 25, 1941. eeoc.gov/eeoc/history/35th/thelaw/eo-8802.html.

19. Harry S. Truman Presidential Library and Museum, "Opinions About Negro Infantry Platoons in White Companies of 7 Divisions," Desegregation of the Armed Forces Research File, July 3, 1945. trumanlibrary.org/whistlestop/study_collections/desegregation/large/documents/index.php?documentid=10-11&pagenumber=3.

20. "Executive Order 9981," July 26, 1948. eeoc.gov/eeoc/history/35th/thelaw/eo-9981.html.

21. "Executive Order 10925," March 6, 1961. eeoc.gov/eeoc/history/35th/thelaw/eo-10925.html.

22. The Civil Rights Acts of 1957 and 1960, while massively important, addressed voting rights issues rather than employment practices and therefore aren't directly related to workplace diversity.

23. Terry Golway and Les Krantz, *JFK: Day by Day: A Chronicle of the 1,036 Days of John F. Kennedy's Presidency* (Philadelphia: Running Press, 2010), p. 284.

24. Robert Dallek, *Lyndon B. Johnson: Portrait of a President* (Oxford: Oxford University Press, 2005), p. 169.

25. "42 U.S. Code § 2000e–2 - Unlawful Employment Practices," July 2, 1964. law.cornell.edu/uscode/text/42/2000e-2.

26. Dana Hull, "Tesla Is a 'Hotbed for Racist Behavior,' Worker Claims in Suit," November 13, 2017. bloomberg.com/news/articles/2017-11-13/tesla-a-hotbed-for-racist-behavior-black-workers-claim-in-suit.

27. Rohini Anand and Mary-Frances Winters. "A Retrospective View of Corporate Diversity Training From 1964 to the Present." *Academy of Management Learning & Education* 7, no. 3 (2008): pp. 356–372. wintersgroup.com/corporate-diversity-training-1964-to-present.pdf (accessed November 2017).

28. Jamison, K. 1978. Affirmative Action program: Springboard for a Total Organizational Change Effort. *OD Practitioner,* 10(4): 1–6.

29. Anand and Winters, "A Retrospective View of Corporate Diversity Training From 1964 to Present."

30. Frank Dobbin and Alexandra Kalev, "Why Diversity Programs Fail," July–August, 2016. hbr.org/2016/07/why-diversity-programs-fail.

31. Hunt, Layton, and Prince, "Why Diversity Matters."

32. Hunt, Layton, and Prince, "Why Diversity Matters."

33. Cedric Hunt, "Is Diversity Still a Good Thing?," *American Sociological Review* 82, no. 4 (2017):868–877. journals.sagepub.com/doi/full/10.1177/0003122417716611 (accessed November 2017).

34. PWC, *17th Annual Global CEO Survey: Transforming talent strategy*, 2014. pwc.com/gx/en/services/people-organisation/publications/ceosurvey-talent-challenge.html.

35. Reid Wilson, "Post-Recession Generation to be Minority-Majority," June 27, 2017. thehill.com/homenews/state-watch/339722-post-recession-generation-to-be-majority-minority#bottom-story-socials.

36. Lisa Frye, "The Cost of a Bad Hire Can Be Astronomical," May 9, 2017. shrm.org/resourcesandtools/hr-topics/employee-relations/pages/cost-of-bad-hires.aspx.

37. Center for American Progress, *"Economic Indicators and People of Color,"* August 2015. cdn.americanprogress.org/wp-content/uploads/2015/08/05075343/PeopleOfColor-Econ-FS.pdf

38. Hunt, "Is Diversity Still a Good Thing?"

39. Hunt, "Is Diversity Still a Good Thing?"

40. Tessa L. Dover, Brenda Major, and Cheryl R. Kaiser, "Diversity Policies Rarely Make Companies Fairer, and They Feel Threatening to White Men," *Harvard Business Review*, January 4, 2016. hbr.org/2016/01/diversity-policies-dont-help-women-or-minorities-and-they-make-white-men-feel-threatened.

41. Kirwan Institute for the Study of Race and Ethnicity, *State of the Science: Implicit Bias Review 2015*. kirwaninstitute.osu.edu/research/understanding-implicit-bias (accessed November 12, 2017).

42. Sendhil Mullainathan, "Racial Bias, Even When We Have Good Intentions," January 3, 2015. nytimes.com/2015/01/04/upshot/the-measuring-sticks-of-racial-bias-html.

43. Heather Boushey and Sarah Jane Glynn, *There Are Significant Business Costs to Replacing Employees*, November 16, 2012. americanprogress.org/wp-content/uploads/2012/11/CostofTurnover.pdf.

44. Ann Bares, "2016 Turnover Rates by Industry," April 21, 2017. compensationforce.com/2017/04/2016-turnover-rates-by-industry.html.

45. Allison Scott, Freada Kapor Klein, and Uriridiakoghene Onovakpuri, "Tech Leavers Study," April 27, 2017. kaporcenter.org/wp-content/uploads/2017/08/TechLeavers2017.pdf.

46. Scott, Klein, and Onovakpuri, "Tech Leavers Study."

47. David Novak, "Recognizing Employees Is the Simplest Way to Improve Morale," May 9, 2016. hbr.org/2016/05/recognizing-employees-is-the-simplest-way-to-improve-morale.

48. Novak, "Recognizing Employees Is the Simplest Way to Improve Morale."

49. "SHRM/Globoforce Survey Reveals Positive Employee Experience Critical to Employee Retention," (Globoforce press release, December 14, 2016). businesswire.com/news/home/20161214005205/en/SHRMGloboforce-Survey-Reveals-Positive-Employee-Experience-Critical.

50. Tess Townsend, "Oprah: The Most Important Thing I've Learned About Branding," November 4, 2015. inc.com/tess-townsend/oprah-the-most-important-thing-ive-learned-about-branding.html.

51. Tom Peters, "The Brand Called You," August 31, 1997. fastcompany.com/28905/brand-called-you.

52. David McNally and Karl Speak, *Be Your Own Brand: A Breakthrough Formula for Standing Out from the Crowd* (Oakland, CA: Berrett–Koehler Publishers, 2011).

53. Peters, "The Brand Called You."

54. 16Personalities, "ENTP Strengths and Weaknesses." 16personalities.com/entp-strengths-and-weaknesses (accessed February 2018).

55. Jeff Beer, "Meet The Agency That Turned MoonPie Into Twitter's Funniest Snack Cake," December 21, 2017. fastcompany.com/40510696/meet-the-agency-that-turned-moonpie-into-twitters-funniest-snack-cake.

56. Julia Greenberg, "Tinder Completely Freaked Out on Twitter," August 11, 2015. wired.com/2015/08/tinder-completely-freaked-twitter.

57. Gwendolyn Seidman, "Is Tinder Really a Hookup App?" June 11, 2017. psychologytoday.com/blog/close-encounters/201706/is-tinder-really-hookup-app.

58. Katherine W. Phillips, Tracy L. Dumas, and Nancy P. Rothbard, "Diversity and Authenticity," March 2018. hbr.org/2018/03/diversity-and-authenticity.

59. Carl Rogers, "A Theory of Therapy, Personality and Interpersonal Relationships as Developed in the Client-centered Framework." In (ed.) S. Koch, *Psychology: A Study of a Science. vol. 3: Formulations of the Person and the Social Context.* (New York: McGraw Hill, 1959).

60. Rogers, "A Theory of Therapy, Personality and Interpersonal Relationships as Developed in the Client-centered Framework."

61. Carl Rogers, *Client-centered Therapy: Its Current Practice, Implications and Theory* (Boston: Houghton Mifflin Company, 1951).

62. Joseph Grenny and David Maxfield, VitalSmarts.com, 2016. vitalsmarts.com/press/2016/05/new-study-shows-its-never-been-riskier-to-talk-about-politics.

63. Elizabeth Kolbert, "Why Facts Don't Change Our Minds," *The New Yorker,* February 27, 2017. www.newyorker.com/magazine/2017/02/27/why-facts-dont-change-our-minds.

64. David Washington, *The Concept of Diversity*, p. 3. dwashingtonllc.com/images/pdf/publications/the concept of diversity.pdf (accessed February 2018).

65. Anna Holmes, "Has 'Diversity' Lost Its Meaning?" October 27, 2015. nytimes.com/2015/11/01/magazine/has-diversity-lost-its-meaning.html.

66. Jennifer Kim, "50+ Ideas for Cultivating Diversity and Inclusion in the Workplace," March 14, 2017. business.linkedin.com/talent-solutions/blog/diversity/2017/50-ideas-for-cultivating-diversity-and-inclusion-in-the-workplace.

67. Anton James Duvall, "Calculating a Mentor's Effect on Salary and Retention," December 1, 2016. fm-magazine.com/issues/2016/dec/mentors-effect-on-salary-and-retention.html.

68. 68. Erika Irish Brown, "Why Employee Resource Groups Still Matter," July 31, 2017. bloomberg.com/diversity-inclusion/blog/employee-resource-groups-still-matter.

69. Arnand and Winters," A Retrospective View of Corporate Diversity Training From 1964 to the Present."

70. "EEOC Issues FY 2017 Performance Report," U.S. Equal Opportunity Employment Commission press release, November 15, 2017, eeoc.gov/eeoc/newsroom/release/11-15-17a.cfm.

71. "EEOC Issues FY 2017 Performance Report."

72. Washington State Office of Financial Management—State Human Resources, "Measuring Diversity." ofm.wa.gov/state-human-resources/diversity/diversity-management/measuring-diversity (accessed March 2017).

73. "Only 1 In 5 New Board Appointees At Fortune 500 Companies Are Not White," *Fortune*. fortune.com/2017/06/19/one-in-5-fortune-500-board-appointees-last-year-was-from-an-underrepresented-group (accessed July 11, 2018).

74. Emily Peck, "Could This Be The Secret to Hiring More Women and People of Color?" *The Huffington Post*, February 10, 2016. huffingtonpost.com/entry/accenture-diversity-referral-bonus_us_56ba334ee4b08ffac122d474 (accessed July 11, 2018).

75. "Collaboration U: Business and University Partnerships to Secure Talent Pipelines," Human Capital Institute, 2015. pcdn1.hci.org/files/field_content_file/2015%20Talent%20Pulse%20TA%20%281%29.pdf (accessed April 2017).

76. Sanjeev Agrawal, "How Companies Can Attract the Best College Talent," *Harvard Business Review*, April 19, 2016. hbr.org/2014/03/how-companies-can-attract-the-best-college-talent (accessed June 1, 2018).

77. Agrawal, "How Companies Can Attract the Best College Talent."

78. Irfan Ahmad, "The Influencer Marketing Revolution," *Social Media Today*, February 16, 2018. socialmediatoday.com/news/the-influencer-marketing-revolution-infographic/517146 (accessed June 9, 2018).

79. "Posse Facts & Figures," About Posse—The Posse Foundation. possefoundation.org/posse-facts (accessed June 8, 2017).

80. "CAREERS," Viacom. viacom.com/about/pages/careers.aspx (accessed April 2, 2018).

81. Nelson Mandela Foundation, " Biography of Nelson Mandela." nelsonmandela.org/content/page/biography (accessed April 2018).

82. Association for Psychological Science, "The Ins and Outs of In-Groups and Out-Groups," November 1, 2012. psychologicalscience.org/news/releases/the-ins-and-outs-of-in-groups-and-out-groups.html.

83. Mary Benson, *Nelson Mandela: The Man and the Movement*, 2nd ed. (New York: WW. Norton & Co., 1994).

84. William H. Frey, "The US Will Become 'minority White' in 2045, Census Projects," *Brookings*, June 29, 2018. brookings .edu/blog/the-avenue/2018/03/14/the-us-will-become-minority-white-in-2045-census-projects (accessed July 11, 2018).

85. "American Demography 2030: Bursting with Diversity, Yet a Baby Bust," *Urban Land* magazine, December 22, 2015. urbanland.uli.org/industry-sectors/american-demography-bursting-diversity-yet-baby-bust (accessed March 3, 2018).

86. Jeffery M. Humphreys, "The Multicultural Economy 2017," Selig Center for Economic Growth, University of Georgia, 2017.

INDEX

P

R

S

 Published in the United States by
Lorena Jones Books, an imprint of the Crown Publishing Group,
a division of Penguin Random House LLC, New York.
www.crownpublishing.com
www.tenspeed.com

Library of Congress Cataloging-in-Publication Data
Names: Braswell, Porter, author.
Title: Let them see you : the guide for leveraging your diversity
at work / Porter Braswell.
Description: First Edition. | California/New York : Lorena Jones Books,
2019. | Includes bibliographical references and index.
Identifiers: LCCN 2018042897 (print) | LCCN 2018045267 (ebook) |
ISBN 9780399581410 (eBook) | ISBN 9780399581403 (hardback)
Subjects: LCSH: Career development. | Personnel management. | Diversity
in the workplace. | BISAC: BUSINESS & ECONOMICS / Careers /
General. | BUSINESS & ECONOMICS / Human Resources &
Personnel Management.
Classification: LCC HF5381 (ebook) | LCC HF5381 .B6393 2019 (print) |
DDC 650.1—dc23
LC record available at https://lccn.loc.gov/2018042897

Hardcover ISBN: 978-0-399-58140-3
Ebook ISBN: 978-0-399-58141-0

Printed in the United States of America

Design by Lisa Schneller Bieser

10 9 8 7 6 5 4 3 2 1

First Edition